THE ULTIMATE
KETO
DIET

INTRODUCTION

WHILE SOME MAY ASSUME IT'S JUST ANOTHER flash-in-the-pan fad, the ketogenic diet has actually been around since the 1920s. Back then, it was one of the most reliable treatment methods for difficult-to-control epilepsy in young children. As anti-seizure medications became more readily available, though, keto went to the wayside as people preferred a quick fix—even if that fix meant the potential for more side effects. Today, people following nutritional ketogenic diets report weight loss, increased energy levels, better moods, improved concentration and mental clarity. And you can too. With this beginner's guide, you'll find everything you need along the way, from the science behind ketosis to a host of delicious recipes, which make sticking to the diet that much easier. Your journey starts now, so let's cook (and burn) some fat!

KETO BEGINNER

Introduction 5

Breakfast 11

Snacks and Fat Bombs 27

Mains 41

Sides 75

Dessert 97

WHAT IS KETO?

Here are the basics you'll need to know when someone inevitably asks, "What exactly is this new diet you're doing?"

FIRST THING'S FIRST: Keto is not just another name for "paleo" or "gluten-free," and it's also not all butter and bacon, as many people tend to assume. Keto is a low-carb lifestyle—meaning those who follow it allow themselves 20 to 50 grams per day—intended to reduce cravings and burn fat. Other than that, the only real rules of this diet are as follows: 1. Eat real food. 2. Stay in ketosis.

The word "keto" comes from the words ketogenic and ketosis (not to be confused with ketoacidosis, which is a concern for diabetics). On this diet, your body will ideally be in a state of ketosis, during which it will create ketones. Because your brain's processes use carbs and sugar, your body simply creates and substitutes ketones when there's an absence of carbohydrates.

Before diving deeper into how your body fuels itself without carbs (page 6) and the science of ketosis (page 8), there's something else about keto that needs to be known right up front: You can't stock up on $1 boxes of pasta anymore, so your grocery bill may rise at first. The reality is that fresh, natural foods are simply pricier (because they're of a much higher quality!). When you go grocery shopping, try to seek out grass-fed, nitrate-free meats and other high-quality proteins whenever possible. As for how you spend the few carbs you can eat, that's entirely up to you, though it's recommend you go for a helping of fibrous veggies, and not a slice of bread, which will spike your blood sugar. All you have to do is keep track of your net carbs, as in the total carbs minus the fiber, for any food you eat. Overall, keto is more customizable than many people might imagine, and you'll inevitably figure out ways to keep the costs down as you get used to it.

Going keto may seem challenging, and that's because it is. But the issues for which it's been used to help—from weight loss to epilepsy to Alzheimer's to cancer—are far more challenging. And not only does keto get easier with a little time, your body will thank you for making the change.

FINDING YOUR FUEL
With carbs nearly absent from your diet, proteins and fats will step up to keep your body going.

YOUR BODY NEEDS ENERGY to keep you alive and doing all the things you want to do. If your body didn't get energy, your cells would starve and the physiological processes that keep you ticking would shut down. In short—you'd die. Your body has a few different tricks it can use to turn the food you eat into energy and keep you alive, but the one it uses most often is to convert the glucose from carbohydrates into fuel. As long as you keep feeding your body carbohydrates, it will convert them into energy, as well as some fat it stores in the process. Carbs are like the gas station closest to your house: convenient, widely accessible, comfortable. But if that gas station closed down, you'd be forced to find fuel elsewhere. Your body is the same way. If you deny it the fuel it needs from carbs, it'll find fuel another way.

FRIENDLY FAT
THOUGH IT'S BEEN VILIFIED for years, fat is not the enemy. Whether big and tall or slim and small, fat is keeping all of us alive. It's an integral part of every cell in your body—from your heart to your lungs to your brain—making up the membranes that hold each cell together. Fat and cholesterol are the building blocks of many different hormones, thereby determining our growth and development, regulating our metabolism and helping us to maintain our bone and muscle mass. It keeps us healthy by maintaining proper immune function, regulating body temperature and insulating our vital organs to protect them from trauma. If you're reading this and thinking, "Wow, maybe I need fat more than I thought," you'd be right. Fat is rightly labeled as an essential nutrient, in part because it plays such a significant role in our bodies' complex systems, and also because our bodies need more fat than they can create on their own. As such, we have to ingest fat to ensure our bodies are working at their peak.

Fat is made up of individual molecules called fatty acids, some of which you've likely heard name-dropped on every "healthy eating" list in the last decade. Omega-3 fatty acids, which play a standout role in proper brain function and development, and omega-6 fatty acids, which help regulate metabolism and affect bone health, are on those lists for a reason. Fat also helps your body absorb some of the other nutrients you need, including vitamins A, D, E and K, as well as beta-carotene. If you aren't consuming enough fat, your body won't absorb these essential nutrients and you'll develop various nutritional deficiencies.

And because each gram of fat contains 9 calories, it can be a useful source of energy—one your body can use with ease and efficiency. Unlike carbs, which your body can only store in small amounts, your body can store an almost unlimited amount of fat to use as energy for later, like when you haven't had a bite for a while or when you're asleep. During these periods, your body burns energy from its fat reserves, a physiological process that serves as the foundation for the ketogenic diet.

CARBS, PROTEIN & FAT: A TALE OF THREE FUELS

YOUR BODY'S DEFAULT method for obtaining energy, and one that is particularly effective, is to turn carbohydrates you've consumed into fuel. This is why many endurance athletes will engage in "carbo-loading" by eating a massive pot of pasta or potatoes the night before a big race—it's the fastest way to store as much glycogen (fuel) in your muscles and liver for a short-term energy boost.

When you eat carbs, they get broken down and converted into glucose, which is then absorbed through the walls of your small intestine. It then enters your bloodstream, which raises your blood's glucose levels. This signals your pancreas to send insulin to pick up the glucose from your blood and shuttle it to your cells so they can use it for energy. Once your cells have had their fill, the excess glucose is converted into glycogen so it can be stowed away in your liver and muscles. But your liver can only store glycogen for up to 24 hours, and it also has a limited storage capacity. The excess glucose is converted into triglycerides, which in turn are stored away in your fat cells.

When you've gone without food for a few hours and your blood sugar begins to drop, your body starts to take advantage of the glycogen stored in your liver and muscles before it seeks out other forms of energy. If you're constantly eating carbs, this cycle will never change, and the overflow energy being stored in your fat cells will never realize its original purpose. Instead, it'll take on a new identity: "love handle" or "paunch" or "the building blocks of a dad bod."

Your body can burn through protein for fuel by breaking it down into individual amino acids, which are then converted into sugars, but in general this is your body's least favorite way to keep itself running. Protein has so many other uses—supporting cell structure, facilitating processes such as digestion and metabolism, transporting oxygen and waste, and acting as antibodies to keep your immune system kicking, to name a few—that burning it to help you walk from your desk to your car is a bit of a waste of potential. Relying on protein to be your body's main source of energy can also lead to a loss of muscle mass alongside other nutritional deficiencies, which is why extremely low-calorie diets can cause more harm than good.

Which leaves us with fat. If it doesn't have carbs to convert into energy, fat is your body's next (and best) choice. The fat from the food you consume gets converted into fatty acids, which eventually make their way into your bloodstream via the small intestine. Most cells in your body can use fatty acids for energy directly, but some cells—such as those in your brain and muscles—can't rely on them unless they are slightly transformed into something scientists call ketones.

KETOSIS 101

To experience the full benefits of the keto diet, your body must enter—and stay in—this state.

WHAT IS KETOSIS?
TO CONVERT FAT INTO ENERGY your whole body can take advantage of, the liver converts it into fatty acids and then transforms those acids into energy-rich substances called ketones or ketone bodies. When these substances are in your blood, you are in a state of ketosis. The goal of a ketogenic diet is to make it so you're in ketosis all the time, turning your body and its various parts into a fat-burning machine.

When following a ketogenic diet, fat is taken to the liver where it is broken down into glycerol and fatty acids through a process called beta-oxidation. The fatty-acid molecules are further broken down through a process called ketogenesis and a specific ketone body called acetoacetate is formed.

Over time, as your body becomes adapted to using ketones as fuel, your muscles convert acetoacetate into beta-hydroxybutyrate, or BHB, which is the preferred source of energy for your brain, and acetone, most of which is expelled from the body as waste. The glycerol created during beta-oxidation goes through a process called gluconeogenesis, where your body converts it into glucose (the same thing it turns carbs into), which it can then use for fuel.

HOW KETOSIS CATALYZES WEIGHT LOSS
IF YOUR BODY IS NO LONGER relying on carbs as its default source of energy, the excess energy created by the conversion process is no longer being stored in fat cells. Additionally, when you're ingesting less carbs, your body is more likely to deplete the energy it stored within your liver and muscles, which means it'll immediately turn to the energy it stored away as triglycerides in your fat cells. When you're on the ketogenic diet, your body is burning the fat you consume for energy, as well as tapping into the energy it has stored away. When your fat cells start providing fuel, they shrink, leading to both a leaner look and noticeable weight loss.

INDUCING KETOSIS
NOW THAT YOU KNOW what it is, the next step is making it happen. The first step is to dramatically decrease the amount of carbohydrates you consume. You also need to limit your protein intake. Traditional low-carb diets typically don't induce ketosis because they allow for a higher amount of protein; if your body converts excess protein into glucose it won't switch over to burning fat for energy. A diet that promotes eating foods with a high-fat diet, a lower amount of protein and a minimal amount of carbs is the right formula for inducing ketosis—and that's what the ketogenic diet is.

The percentage of each macronutrient required to kick-start the process of ketosis varies from person to person, but in general the ratios fall into the following ranges:

- 5–10 percent of calories from carbohydrates
- 15–30 percent of calories from protein
- 60–75 percent of calories from fat

Once you find yourself in ketosis, you'll want to stick with the keto diet, maintaining similar ratios of fat to protein to carbs, otherwise your body will get too much glucose from what you're ingesting and will no longer need to burn fat as fuel.

GUT CHECK: THE KETO FLU

WHILE IT'S NOT PRECISE in terms of nomenclature, given that the ketogenic diet doesn't lead to any form of influenza, its potential side effects will likely be incredibly (and uncomfortably) familiar to anyone who's been waylaid by the flu. Basic symptoms include headaches and fatigue, but some extreme, rare cases may include nausea, upset stomach, abdominal cramps and diarrhea as your body is going through carbohydrate withdrawal.

Carb addiction is a real phenomenon, and some research has shown carbohydrates activate stimuli in the brain that can be dependence-forming. Carb addicts experience uncontrollable cravings for carbs and tend to binge when they get the chance. For a carb addict, the sudden cessation of a regular dose of carbohydrates can cause withdrawal symptoms, including dizziness, irritability and intense cravings.

The amount of time it takes for the keto flu to subside varies, but it shouldn't last longer than two weeks and typically fades away in less than half that time. A good way to ward off this unpleasant experience is to drink homemade bone broth. Many of the symptoms of keto flu are associated with dehydration since during the beginning stages of ketosis you shed a lot of water weight and electrolytes. Replenishing those resources will get your body back on track, and homemade bone broth can help lessen the severity of any symptoms you're experiencing. Though the keto flu will affect some worse than others, it's important to acknowledge that it'll likely impact you in some way—the key is to push through and recognize that the benefits of the diet will far outweigh the negatives it takes to see them take effect.

Breakfast

YOU'LL BE READY TO FACE WHATEVER THE DAY THROWS AT YOU WITH THESE INNERVATING, INVENTIVE KETO-CENTRIC TWISTS ON CLASSIC A.M. FARE.

FARMER'S EGG BAKE
with Garlic Parmesan Gravy

Get ready for this easy breakfast bake you can make the night before, using staples you likely already have in your refrigerator. In the morning, simply whip up the Garlic Parmesan Gravy, toss and enjoy! This recipe is best and most keto-friendly when you buy your meats local so they're less processed; however, as long as you check your nutrition labels, all of these meats can be found at your local grocery store.

PREP TIME 15–20 MINUTES **COOK TIME** 4 HOURS ON HIGH OR 6–8 HOURS ON LOW **YIELD** 13 SERVINGS **SERVING** 1 CUP **SLOW COOKER SIZE** 6-QUART

INGREDIENTS
EGG BAKE
- 12 large eggs
- 1 cup cubed ham
- 14 oz kielbasa or Polish sausage, cut into slices
- ½ lb pre-cooked ground Italian sausage
- 1 green bell pepper, cored and chopped
- 1 red bell pepper, cored and chopped
- 1 small yellow onion, chopped
- 2 cups chopped cauliflower, bite-size
- 2 cups shredded cheddar cheese
- cup salted butter, melted
- Tbsp freshly ground black pepper

GARLIC PARMESAN GRAVY
- 2 Tbsp ghee or butter
- 2 tsp minced garlic
- ½ cup chicken broth
- 1½ cups heavy cream
- ½ cup grated real Parmesan cheese
- Salt and pepper, to taste

INSTRUCTIONS

1. Grease your slow cooker, then crack the eggs into it and use a whisk to scramble well. Add the rest of the egg bake ingredients, then use a wooden spoon or spatula to mix together well. Cook on high for 4 hours or on low overnight in a programmable slow cooker for 6 to 8 hours.

2. In the morning, use a wooden spoon to "scramble" the mixture and break it up, then make the gravy on the stove—it's worth the time and best done right before serving. To make the gravy, preheat a medium skillet to medium and melt the ghee or butter, then sizzle the garlic for about 30 seconds, or until fragrant. Add chicken broth and heavy cream, then keep at a lively simmer until the sauce has reduced in half and covers a spoon in a thick sauce (about 10 minutes). Remove from heat, add the Parmesan and mix until melted (must be real Parmesan cheese), then add a generous amount of salt and pepper to taste.

3. Serve your egg bake drizzled in gravy, or add to slow cooker scramble and toss.

PER SERVING Net Carbs: 6g | Calories: 483 | Fat: 39g | Carbs: 7g | Protein: 22g | Fiber: 1g

KETO BREAKFAST SANDWICH

Instead of English muffins or fake muffins, you'll be using two eggs to create the perfect top and bottom for all your fillings.

PREP TIME 15 MINUTES **YIELD** 1 SANDWICH **SERVING** 1

INGREDIENTS

- 1 Tbsp ghee or butter
- 2 large eggs
- 1 slice Gouda cheese (cheddar also works)
- 1 slice bacon (cooked)
- 2 thin slices avocado
- ¼ cup arugula
- 1 tsp prepared garlic aioli
- Salt and pepper

INSTRUCTIONS

1. Grease two rings with butter or olive oil so the egg doesn't stick to it when you try to remove it later.

2. Preheat your skillet to medium and melt 1 tablespoon ghee or butter.

3. Place the rings down and crack one egg into each. Sprinkle with a pinch of salt and pepper on each. Cover to cook all the way through more quickly. Yolks should not be runny.

4. Remove from the rings and sear one last time on both sides, about 30 seconds each. Place cheese on one egg and cover until it melts.

5. Now begin plating, starting with your naked egg, folded bacon, avocado, arugula and garlic aioli. Top with your second egg, cheese facing down, and serve.

PER SERVING Net Carbs: 3g | Calories: 524 | Fat: 46g | Carbs: 6g | Protein: 23g | Fiber: 3g

Easy **GIANT WESTERN OMELET**

This breakfast uses traditional Western omelet ingredients like ham, peppers and onions, then adds ghee as a keto-friendly fat to create an extra-savory meal. If you'd like, substitute ham for grilled or rotisserie chicken and add a teaspoon of smoked paprika to switch it up!

PREP TIME 10 MINUTES **COOK TIME** 2 HOURS ON HIGH OR 4–6 HOURS ON LOW **YIELD** 8 SLICES **SERVING** 1 SLICE **SLOW COOKER SIZE** 6-QUART

INGREDIENTS
- 6 Tbsp ghee or butter, melted, divided
- 10 large eggs
- ¾ cup heavy cream
- ¼ tsp salt
- ⅛ tsp freshly ground black pepper
- ½ small (2") jalapeño pepper, deseeded, diced
- ½ cup chopped green bell pepper, (about green pepper)
- ½ cup chopped yellow onion, (about ½ medium onion)
- 1 cup cubed ham
- 1 cup shredded cheddar cheese

INSTRUCTIONS
1. Use 2 tablespoons ghee or butter to grease your slow cooker.
2. In a bowl, whisk together eggs, heavy cream, salt and pepper. Add in the peppers, onion, ham, cheese and remaining ghee and mix.
3. Pour into the greased slow cooker and cook on high for 2 hours or on low for at least 4 hours, but no longer than 6 hours.

PER SERVING Net Carbs: 3g | Calories: 340 | Fat: 30g | Carbs: 3g | Protein: 15g | Fiber: 0g

SCRAMBLED EGGNOG

A twist on scrambled eggs, this dish is almost as sweet as it is savory. It draws in natural sweetness from cinnamon and cream cheese, and can be taken a step sweeter with a couple drops of stevia glycerite—the non-bitter version of stevia.

PREP TIME 5 MINUTES **YIELD** 4 **SERVING** 1 CUP

INGREDIENTS

- 6 slices bacon
- 1 cup shelled, halved walnuts, unsalted
- 8 large eggs
- 6 Tbsp cream cheese
- 4 Tbsp heavy whipping cream
- 3 tsp coconut flour
- ½ tsp ground cinnamon
- ⅛ tsp nutmeg
- Pinch of salt
- 1 tsp vanilla extract
- 1 Tbsp ghee (or butter)
- 2 drops stevia glycerite (optional)

INSTRUCTIONS

1. Preheat oven to 400 degrees F.

2. On a baking sheet, lay out the bacon evenly across the pan (you'll be adding walnuts to the pan soon). Bake for 10 minutes, then remove from the oven, toss in the walnuts and turn them so they're covered in bacon grease, then sprinkle the whole tray with a light layer of cinnamon.

3. Bake for another 10 minutes, or until crispy. Toss together again, remove to drain on a paper towel, cool, then crumble together in a separate bowl.

4. In a blender, combine the eggs, cream cheese, heavy whipping cream, coconut flour, ground cinnamon, nutmeg, salt, vanilla and Stevia Glycerite. Blend until well-mixed.

5. In a medium skillet, melt the ghee over medium heat. Add the egg mixture and, using a spatula, gently flip and scramble every 30 seconds or so until the eggs are cooked through and no longer runny.

6. When done, plate and top with the bacon and walnut mixture as garnish. Serve alone topped with butter or add sugar-free, keto-friendly maple syrup.

PER SERVING Net Carbs: 4g | Calories: 459 | Fat: 40g | Carbs: 6g | Protein: 20g | Fiber: 2g

LEMON POPPY SEED BREAD
with Cream Cheese Drizzle

This baked Lemon Poppy Seed Bread is easy to make and tastes just like the muffins you've been missing. You can also use the batter for your other favorite muffins, like blueberry, for 17 grams net carbs per cup—or less than 1 gram per serving in this recipe.

PREP TIME 10 MINUTES **COOK TIME** 4 HOURS ON HIGH OR 6 HOURS ON LOW **YIELD** 20 SLICES **SERVING** 1 SLICE **SLOW COOKER SIZE** 6-QUART

INGREDIENTS

- 4 cups almond flour
- 2 cups powdered erythritol, divided
- 2 Tbsp poppy seeds
- 2 tsp baking powder
- ½ tsp salt
- 5 eggs
- 1 cup heavy cream
- 1 cup unsalted butter, melted
- 4 lemons (zest and juice)
- ½ cup cream cheese, melted
- 2 drops stevia glycerite
- ½ tsp vanilla extract

INSTRUCTIONS

1. In a bowl, combine the dry ingredients first: almond flour, 1 cup erythritol, poppy seeds, baking powder and salt. In a second bowl, whisk together the eggs and heavy cream.

2. Combine the two bowls with a spatula until smooth, then mix in the melted butter and finally the lemon juice and zest.

3. Line your slow cooker with tinfoil (plastic liners won't work here) so it's easier to remove when you're done, then grease. Pour batter into the slow cooker and cook on high for 4 hours or on low for 6 hours. Rotate the slow cooker dish halfway through cooking to help it cook evenly.

4. Let cool completely and refrigerate in the slow cooker overnight.

5. In the morning, remove from the slow cooker, slice horizontally, then vertically into slices to make 20 total slices. Mix together the melted cream cheese, remaining 1 cup erythritol, stevia and vanilla extract, then drizzle over the bread generously and serve. This also tastes great reheated with butter.

PER SERVING Net Carbs: 3g | Calories: 287 | Fat: 26g | Carbs: 6g | Protein: 7g | Fiber: 3g

Crunchy TOASTED NUT CINNAMON GRANOLA

Replace cereal with a healthy mix of unsweetened coconut flakes, almonds and walnuts dressed in cinnamon and stevia.

PREP TIME 5 MINUTES **YIELD** 3 CUPS **SERVING** 4

INGREDIENTS

- ¼ cup almond slices
- ¼ cup chopped walnuts
- 2½ cups unsweetened coconut flakes
- 2 tsp ground cinnamon
- 2 Tbsp coconut oil, melted
- 2 drops stevia glycerite

INSTRUCTIONS

1. Preheat oven to 375 degrees F and line a baking sheet with parchment paper.
2. In a medium bowl, toss the nuts and coconut flakes with the melted coconut oil, then the cinnamon and sweetener.
3. Spread out the mixture over the baking sheet in as close to a single layer as you can.
4. Add to the oven and bake for about 10 minutes, or until the mixture begins to brown (keep an eye on it; oven times may vary).
5. Remove, shuffle and toss, then let cool. Enjoy alone or serve in a bowl with unsweetened almond milk, or atop unsweetened full-fat Greek yogurt or quark.
6. To store, add to a zipper storage bag with a paper towel to absorb any moisture.

PER SERVING Net Carbs: 1g | Calories: 320 | Fat: 29g | Carbs: 8g | Protein: 5g | Fiber: 7g

Slow Cooker BREAKFAST SAUSAGE

Serve this breakfast sausage alongside some hot, buttery eggs for a complete keto-friendly breakfast. This savory pork sausage is laced with liquid smoke and maple extract for a traditional hot-off-the-skillet taste, and it's best cooked slowly.

PREP TIME 10 MINUTES **COOK TIME** 4–6 HOURS ON LOW **YIELD** 8 SAUSAGES **SERVING** 1 SAUSAGE **SLOW COOKER SIZE** 6-QUART

INGREDIENTS
- 3 lb ground pork
- 2 Tbsp chopped fresh sage (or 1 Tbsp dried)
- 2 Tbsp chopped fresh thyme (or 1 Tbsp dried)
- 1 Tbsp maple extract
- 6 drops stevia glycerite
- ⅛ tsp allspice
- ½ tsp red pepper flakes
- 1 Tbsp fennel seeds
- 1 Tbsp salt
- ½ tsp freshly ground black pepper
- ¼ tsp liquid smoke (optional)

INSTRUCTIONS
In a bowl, mix all ingredients together thoroughly, then press into the bottom of a greased slow cooker. Cook on low for at least 4 hours and up to 6 hours.

PER SERVING Net Carbs: 0g | Calories: 303 | Fat: 24g | Carbs: 1g | Protein: 19g | Fiber: 1g

Crustless BROCCOLI CHEDDAR QUICHE

Imagine a pan of fragrant shallots sizzling in bacon drippings and tossed with fresh broccoli—that's how this broccoli quiche recipe starts. It only gets better when you cover it with a savory layer of Dijon whisked eggs and bake to fluffy, savory perfection!

PREP TIME 20 MINUTES **YIELD** 10 SLICES
SERVING 1 SLICE

INGREDIENTS

- 2 Tbsp ghee, divided
- 5 large eggs
- 1 cup heavy cream
- 1 Tbsp Dijon mustard
- 1 pinch cinnamon
- 8 oz bacon, chopped
- 1 small head broccoli, chopped (3 cups)
- 2 shallots, peeled and diced (½ cup)
- ½ cup chicken broth
- 1 cup shredded cheddar cheese

INSTRUCTIONS

1. Preheat oven to 375 degrees F and grease a 9-inch glass pie plate with 1 tablespoon ghee.
2. In a mixing bowl, whisk together the eggs, heavy cream, Dijon mustard and cinnamon. Set aside.
3. In a medium skillet over medium heat, cook the bacon to a light crisp, about 5 minutes.
4. Remove the bacon from the skillet but leave the bacon grease. Add the last tablespoon of ghee and melt, then add the shallots and cook for about 2 minutes, being careful not to burn.
5. Add the chicken broth and broccoli and cook until soft and broth has evaporated, which should occur around the same time.
6. Pour into the pie plate and arrange so it's even all the way around, then pour the egg mixture over the top. It should be the perfect amount, but if there's more, discard the extra.
7. Sprinkle with the cheddar, then bake for 30 minutes, or until the center is between 160 and 180 degrees F and a knife comes out clean when you poke the center.
8. Remove from the oven and allow to cool for about 15 minutes, then serve.

PER SERVING Net Carbs: 3g | Calories: 313 | Fat: 27g | Carbs: 4g | Protein: 15g | Fiber: 1g

Slow Cooker
CREAM CHEESE COFFEE CAKE

Coffee cake is one of the best pairings for your morning coffee, so why give it up on keto? Baked goods aren't for every day, but you can enjoy them for special occasions. For an overnight treat that's ready in the morning, cook on low in a programmable slow cooker for 6 hours instead.

PREP TIME 10 MINUTES **COOK TIME** 2–3 HOURS ON HIGH OR 6 HOURS ON LOW **YIELD** 15 SLICES **SERVING** 1 SLICE **SLOW COOKER SIZE** 7-QUART

INGREDIENTS

COFFEE CAKE
- 9 Tbsp unsalted butter, room-temperature, divided
- 2 cups finely ground almond flour
- 1 cup flaxseed flour or coconut flour
- 1 cup powdered erythritol
- 2 Tbsp ground cinnamon
- 1 Tbsp nutmeg
- 2 Tbsp baking powder
- 1 tsp baking soda
- 1 tsp salt
- 4 eggs
- 2 Tbsp vanilla extract
- 6 drops stevia glycerite
- 4 oz cream cheese, softened
- 1 cup sour cream

CINNAMON CRUMBLE
- 1 cup almond flour
- 1 cup granulated erythritol
- 8 Tbsp unsalted butter, cold
- ½ Tbsp cinnamon

INSTRUCTIONS

1. Line the slow cooker with foil and grease the bottom and lower third using 1 tablespoon butter.
2. In a bowl, combine dry ingredients (almond flour, flaxseed or coconut flour, erythritol, ground cinnamon, nutmeg, baking powder, baking soda and salt).
3. Using a hand mixer, add the eggs, then mix. Add the rest of the wet ingredients (remaining butter, vanilla, stevia glycerite, cream cheese and sour cream) and blend with a hand mixer.
4. Cook in the slow cooker on high for 2 to 3 hours or on low for 6 hours. Rotate halfway through to avoid burning on one side.
5. In a separate bowl, combine streusel ingredients (almond flour, erythritol and cinnamon). Slice butter into eighths. Using your hands or a fork, scrunch together in a bowl to create pea-sized crumbles, then sprinkle over the top 1 hour before you're ready to serve.
6. Let cool, lift out of the slow cooker using foil, then slice into 15 pieces (two slices horizontally, four down) and serve.

PER SERVING Net Carbs: 5g | Calories: 331 | Fat: 30g | Carbs: 8g | Protein: 8g | Fiber: 3g

Buttery SCRAMBLED EGGS

Butter and eggs are a classic pairing for a ketogenic breakfast, and this recipe uses the more refined version of butter: ghee!

PREP TIME 1 MINUTE **YIELD** 4 CUPS **SERVING** 1 CUP

INGREDIENTS

- 8 large eggs
- 3 Tbsp ghee (or butter)
- Salt and pepper to taste

INSTRUCTIONS

1. In a bowl, whisk together eggs until well-mixed.
2. Over medium-low heat, melt the ghee, then add the egg mixture and a pinch of salt and pepper.
3. Cook slowly and gently fold the edges as the egg cooks, being careful not to chop with your spatula, but gently moving the eggs around until they're soft and fluffy. Serve hot.

PER SERVING Net Carbs: 1g | Calories: 244 | Fat: 21g | Carbs: 1g | Protein: 13g | Fiber: 0g

CAULIFLOWER HOME FRIES

Prepare keto-friendly home "fries" that are rich in flavor and low in carbs. Cauliflower—and radishes!—are some of the best keto-friendly potato substitutes. Store for breakfasts all week long, and serve it as a side with buttery fried eggs.

PREP TIME 15 MINUTES **COOK TIME** 2–3 HOURS ON HIGH OR 6 HOURS ON LOW **YIELD** 4 CUPS **SERVING** ½ CUP **SLOW COOKER SIZE** 6-QUART

INGREDIENTS

- 1 medium head (5–7") fresh cauliflower, chopped (bite-size for high temp, larger for low temp)
- 6 Tbsp butter, melted
- 16 oz bacon, precooked, crumbled and grease reserved
- ½ cup green chilies, chopped
- 1 small yellow onion, finely diced
- 1 clove garlic, minced
- 1 tsp Cajun seasoning
- ½ tsp paprika
- 1 tsp salt
- ½ tsp freshly cracked black pepper
- Fresh chives, for garnish

INSTRUCTIONS

1. Preheat the slow cooker to high and add in the cauliflower, then toss with the butter and bacon grease. Next, add in the rest of the ingredients and mix.
2. Cook on high for 2 to 3 hours (preferred) or on low for 6 hours. The longer you plan to cook them, the larger the cauliflower pieces should be. You can chop into smaller bites before serving or storing.

PER SERVING Net Carbs: 3g | Calories: 183 | Fat: 15g | Carbs: 5g | Protein: 5g | Fiber: 2g

BREAKFAST CASSEROLE

Your whole family doesn't need to be eating keto to enjoy this breakfast casserole, which is loaded with all your favorite breakfast fixings. It makes enough to feed the whole gang, or you can make it as a food prep meal and eat it all week long.

PREP TIME 35 MINUTES **YIELD** 12 SLICES
SERVING 1 SLICE

INGREDIENTS

- 1 (8-oz) pkg bacon
- ½ cup chopped red bell pepper
- ½ cup chopped onion
- 2 lb ground sausage
- 12 large eggs
- 1 tsp salt
- ½ cup heavy cream
- ½ tsp freshly ground black pepper
- 2 cups cheddar cheese

INSTRUCTIONS

1. Preheat oven to 375 degrees F.
2. In a skillet over medium-high heat, cook the bacon to crisp, cool, then crumble and set aside.
3. Using the same skillet with the bacon grease, sizzle the chopped red peppers and onions for about 3 minutes, or until soft, then add the sausage to the skillet and brown into crumbles.
4. In a large bowl, combine the eggs, heavy cream, salt and pepper. Scramble with a whisk until smooth.
5. In a 9-by-13-inch baking dish, add the sausage mixture to the bottom, then a cup of shredded cheddar, the crumbled bacon and the egg mixture. Bake for at least 30 minutes (ovens will vary), or until cooked through. The eggs may take longer to firm in different ovens. Add the remaining cup of shredded cheddar and bake until melted. Serve.

PER SERVING Net Carbs: 2g | Calories: 521 | Fat: 43g | Carbs: 2g | Protein: 30g | Fiber: 0g

ORANGE BUTTER CREAM CINNAMON ROLLS

Bite into these sweet and pillowy cinnamon rolls that draw in the essence of oranges through zest without splurging on unnecessary sugars. Not only are these sweet and savory cinnamon rolls packed with fats to start your day, they are also drizzled in a sweet orange glaze.

PREP TIME 25 MINUTE **YIELD** 8 ROLLS
SERVING 1 ROLL

INGREDIENT
ROLLS
- 1 cup extra-fine almond flour
- 1 egg
- ½ tsp baking powder
- 1 tsp vanilla
- Zest of 1 orange
- 1 pinch salt
- 2 cups shredded mozzarella
- 2 Tbsp butter
- 2 oz cream cheese

CINNAMON FILLING
- ½ cup butter, softened
- 2 Tbsp cinnamon
- 4 Tbsp sugar-free vanilla sweetener or sugar-free brown sugar sweetener

GLAZE
- ½ cup Swerve® (confectioners)
- ¼ cup butter (room temperature)
- Zest of 1 orange
- ¼ tsp orange extract
- ¼ tsp vanilla extract
- 3 Tbsp heavy cream

INSTRUCTIONS

1. Preheat oven to 350 degrees F.
2. In a bowl, combine the almond flour, egg, baking powder, vanilla, orange zest and salt to create the dough base ingredients.
3. In a second bowl, combine the butter, cinnamon and erythritol filling ingredients and mix until thoroughly blended.
4. In a small saucepan over medium heat, begin to make the dough by melting 2 tablespoons butter, then adding the mozzarella cheese and cream cheese.
5. After about 5 minutes of mixing with a strong wooden spatula, the cheeses will bind together into a smooth batter. Remove from heat and add the almond flour mixture you made earlier. Mix again with a strong wooden spatula until completely blended and can form into a dough ball.
6. Using your hands, press the batter into a flat, uniform 10-by-14-inch rectangle on a piece of parchment paper,

then spread the cinnamon filling evenly across. This will become the swirl in the middle of your cinnamon buns.

7. Lift the edges of your dough from one side of the parchment and proceed to roll into a tube. Roll it the short way instead of the long way. This will make a shorter roll, but you'll have many more swirls of cinnamon. When finished rolling, use the parchment to wrap the roll tightly to keep its shape while it cools in the freezer for 15 minutes.

8. Round out the roll if it flattened in the freezer, then unroll the parchment and use a sharp knife to slice the roll into eight large or 12 small single rolls, and place in a greased 9-inch pie plate spaced evenly apart. Bake for 20 minutes at 350 degrees F.

9. Meanwhile, combine your glaze ingredients, starting with creaming the butter and erythritol together, then adding the orange zest, orange extract, vanilla extract and heavy cream one at a time.

10. When the cinnamon rolls are ready and slightly cooled, drizzle the glaze over the rolls and serve.

PER SERVING Net Carbs: 2g | Calories: 325 | Fat: 34g | Carbs: 5g | Protein: 5g | Fiber: 3g

Snacks & Fat Bombs

KEEP YOURSELF ON THE KETOSIS TRAIN BY ENSURING THESE "IN BETWEEN BITES" ARE ALL ABOARD.

BUFFALO CHICKEN BITES

These buffalo chicken balls are a great party snack for barbecues and birthday parties. Double the recipe for a crowd or make them alone for snacks throughout the week, with a side of blue cheese dressing for dipping. Stores well in the refrigerator for up to a week.

PREP TIME 5 MINUTES **COOK TIME** 2 HOURS ON HIGH OR 6–8 HOURS ON LOW **YIELD** 20 BALLS
SERVING 4 BALLS **SLOW COOKER SIZE** 6-QUART

INGREDIENTS

- 1 cup salted butter, melted
- 1 cup hot sauce
- 1 garlic clove, minced
- 1 tsp smoked paprika
- 1½ tsp salt, divided
- 1½ tsp freshly ground black pepper, divided
- ½ tsp cayenne pepper
- 1 lb ground chicken
- 1 large egg
- 1 cup shredded mozzarella cheese
- ½ cup crumbled blue cheese
- ¼ cup chopped celery
- 2 Tbsp water
- 1 tsp onion powder

INSTRUCTIONS

1. In the slow cooker, add the butter, hot sauce, garlic, paprika, 1 teaspoon salt, 1 teaspoon pepper and cayenne pepper and set to low.

2. In a large bowl, combine the chicken, egg, mozzarella, blue cheese, celery, water, onion powder, and remaining salt and pepper. Use your hands to mix the ingredients well, then wet your hands to keep the balls from sticking and form into about twenty 1-inch meatballs.

3. Add to the slow cooker and cook on low for 6 to 8 hours. To reduce cook time, brown the meatballs in a skillet with olive oil over medium-high heat, then add the meatballs to the slow cooker on high for 2 hours.

PER SERVING Net Carbs: 2g | Calories: 340 | Fat: 17g | Carbs: 2g | Protein: 4g | Fiber: 0g

CHEESE BURGER DIP

This dip tastes just like a hot, gooey cheeseburger from your favorite burger place. It's a perfect party snack and marvelous on veggie sticks, flax crackers, pork rinds and even pickles.

PREP TIME 15 MINUTES **COOK TIME** 3 HOURS ON LOW **YIELD** 8 CUPS **SERVING** 1 CUP **SLOW COOKER SIZE** 6-QUART

INGREDIENTS

- 12 oz bacon, chopped
- 2 lb grass-fed ground beef
- 1 small yellow onion, chopped
- 8 oz cream cheese, cubed
- 4 Tbsp low-sugar ketchup
- 4 Tbsp mustard
- 1 cup chili-ready diced tomatoes
- ½ tsp salt
- ½ tsp freshly ground black pepper
- 3 cups shredded cheddar cheese

GARNISH
- Red onions, chopped
- Sesame seeds

INSTRUCTIONS

1. In a skillet over medium-high heat, cook the bacon, then add onions and cook about 1 minute, then add the ground beef and brown. Add to the slow cooker.

2. Add cream cheese, ketchup, mustard, tomatoes, salt, pepper and 1 cup cheddar cheese. Mix gently.

3. Top with remaining 2 cups cheddar cheese and cook on low for 3 hours. Set to warm, garnish and serve.

PER SERVING Net Carbs: 2g | Calories: 441 | Fat: 34g | Carbs: 2g | Protein: 32g | Fiber: 0g

CHICKEN JALAPEÑO POPPER DIP

Great for parties, this dip tastes just like the appetizer we all know and love at our favorite restaurants. The addition of shredded chicken makes it great for a dip or a meal that you can pack all week long.

PREP TIME 10 MINUTES **COOK TIME** 2 HOURS ON LOW **YIELD** 6 CUPS **SERVING** ½ CUP **SLOW COOKER SIZE** 6-QUART

INGREDIENTS

- 5 jalapeño peppers
- 1 large rotisserie chicken, shredded (3–5 lb or 4–6 cups of meat)
- 16 oz cream cheese, cubed
- 1 cup mayonnaise
- 1 cup shredded cheddar cheese
- 1 tsp garlic powder
- ⅛ tsp salt
- ⅛ tsp freshly ground black pepper
- 1 cup crispy crumbled bacon

GARNISH
- Jalapeño, chopped
- Scallions
- Bacon

SERVE WITH: Fork, celery sticks, pork rinds

INSTRUCTIONS

1. Chop your jalapeños, leaving seeds intact for one of them and removing from the others. (Note: You can also leave more, depending on how spicy you want the dip to be.)

2. Add all ingredients except bacon into the slow cooker and mix, then cook on low for 2 hours or until bubbly. Top with crispy crumbled bacon, then serve.

PER SERVING Net Carbs: 2g | Calories: 424 | Fat: 42g | Carbs: 2g | Protein: 24g | Fiber: 0g

Supreme PIZZA DIP

This adaptable recipe is easy to tailor to your favorite pizza flavors.

PREP TIME 15 MINUTES **COOK TIME** 1–2 HOURS ON HIGH **YIELD** 6 CUPS **SERVING** ½ CUP **SLOW COOKER SIZE** 6-QUART

INGREDIENTS

- 2 lb ground Italian sausage
- 15 oz marinara sauce (keto-friendly)
- 2 cups shredded whole-milk mozzarella cheese
- ½ cup chopped green bell pepper
- ½ cup chopped onion

ADDITIONAL TOPPINGS

- Tomatoes
- Black olives
- Basil

INSTRUCTIONS

1. In a skillet over medium-high heat, add the ground sausage and brown until cooked through. Strain the excess fat and add to the slow cooker.

2. Add marinara sauce and mix. Top with mozzarella cheese, then green peppers and onions and any other fixings you like.

3. Slow cook on high for 1 to 2 hours, then set to warm and serve.

PER SERVING Net Carbs: 3g | Calories: 367 | Fat: 7g | Carbs: 25g | Protein: 28g | Fiber: 4g

GARLIC PARMESAN WINGS

These garlicky wings will transport your taste buds to another world, and they're so easy to make that you could make them for dinner, football games or anytime you want!

PREP TIME 15 MINUTES **COOK TIME** 2 HOURS ON HIGH, THEN 2 HOURS ON LOW **YIELD** 25 WINGS **SERVING** 5 WINGS **SLOW COOKER SIZE** 6-QUART

INGREDIENTS

- 25 fresh chicken wings (drums and flats)
- 6 Tbsp butter or ghee, melted
- 2 cups fresh grated Parmesan, divided
- 5 garlic cloves, minced
- ¼ tsp onion powder
- Pinch of red pepper flakes
- ¼ tsp salt
- ¼ tsp freshly ground black pepper

GARNISH
Freshly chopped parsley

INSTRUCTIONS

1. In the slow cooker, toss the wings with melted butter, 1 cup Parmesan, garlic, onion powder, red pepper flakes, salt and pepper. Cook on high for 2 hours, then on low for 2 hours.

2. Preheat your oven to broil, then line a baking sheet and spread the chicken out. Sprinkle with half the remaining Parmesan cheese and broil for 5 to 10 minutes until crispy. Toss with the last of the Parmesan cheese and freshly chopped parsley. Serve.

PER SERVING Net Carbs: 1g | Calories: 609 | Fat: 49g | Carbs: 1g | Protein: 40g | Fiber: 0g

SWISS FONDUE

When preparing meals for a group, it's always fun to start with some fondue for dipping. You can mix your favorite keto dippables with some average-joe favorites like crackers for your non-keto guests to make everyone happy!

PREP TIME 10 MINUTES **COOK TIME** 1 HOUR ON HIGH, THEN 1 HOUR ON LOW **YIELD** 4 CUPS **SERVING** ¾ CUP **SLOW COOKER SIZE** 2–2.5-QUART

INGREDIENTS

- 1 cup chicken broth
- 2 cups Gruyère cheese, shredded
- 2 cups Swiss cheese, shredded
- 2 tsp xanthan gum
- ½ tsp nutmeg
- ¼ tsp salt
- ⅛ tsp freshly ground black pepper
- Pinch cayenne pepper

INSTRUCTIONS

1. Rub the inside of the slow cooker with a halved garlic clove, then add it to the slow cooker. Add chicken broth and set to high for about 30 minutes.

2. Once hot, remove the garlic clove and add the cheese, xanthan gum, nutmeg, salt and pepper. Mix and cook on high for 30 minutes, then stir and set to low. Let cook until everything looks good and melty (another 30 minutes to 1 hour, stirring frequently), set to warm and serve.

PER SERVING Net Carbs: 1g | Calories: 368 | Fat: 28g | Carbs: 2g | Protein: 26g | Fiber: 1g

PEPPERMINT PATTIES

These minty morsels will melt in your mouth while keeping you in ketosis, thanks to their coconut oil middles. This recipe requires a silicone candy mold with twelve 1-inch circles.

PREP TIME 30 MINUTES **YIELD** 12 PATTIES
SERVING 2 PATTIES

INGREDIENTS

- ½ cup coconut oil (solid)
- 2 tsp vanilla extract, divided
- 1 Tbsp peppermint extract
- 1 Tbsp heavy cream
- 2 Tbsp powdered erythritol, divided
- 4 oz baker's chocolate
- 6 Tbsp unsalted butter

INSTRUCTIONS

1. Over low heat in a small saucepan or in the microwave, melt the coconut oil, then add the vanilla extract, peppermint extract, heavy cream and 1 tablespoon erythritol and whisk until smooth. Place the silicone candy mold on top of a small metal baking sheet that will fit in your freezer. Pour ½ tablespoon of the liquid into each mold, then freeze on top of the baking sheet for at least 20 minutes.

2. On the stove or in the microwave, melt the chocolate then add butter until both the chocolate and butter melt completely. Slowly pour in 1 tablespoon erythritol, whisking as you go to keep it smooth, then add the remaining vanilla and stir—it should be completely smooth.

3. Remove the mold and baking sheet from the freezer. Place parchment paper on the chilled baking sheet and, using a spoon, create twelve 1-inch-thin chocolate circles that will serve as the bottom of your peppermint patties. Top with the coconut-mint fillings, then drizzle chocolate over the tops to finish off your candies. Refreeze quickly to harden, then store in the refrigerator. Enjoy as fat-filled snacks and mini desserts.

PER SERVING Net Carbs: 1g | Calories: 306 | Fat: 33g | Carbs: 2g | Protein: 1g | Fiber: 1g

No-Bake BROWN BUTTER FUDGE BITES

Blended with vanilla and cream cheese, you'll find yourself happy to snack on these simple treats between meals and when you need a boost.

PREP TIME 10 MINUTES **YIELD** 16 BITES
SERVING 2 BITES

INGREDIENTS
- 1 cup unsalted butter
- 16 oz cream cheese, cubed
- 4 Tbsp granulated erythritol
- 2 Tbsp vanilla extract
- Pinch of salt
- Berries, optional

INSTRUCTIONS
1. Line a small baking sheet (9-by-13-inch) with parchment paper, or use a smaller baking dish for a smaller, thicker batch. In a medium saucepan over medium heat, melt the butter and cook for up to 5 minutes, or until the butter begins to darken, then immediately remove from heat.
2. Add the cream cheese and use a hand mixer to blend together. Add the erythritol, vanilla extract and salt and blend until smooth.
3. Pour the mixture into the baking sheet, then refrigerate for 4 hours. Cut into squares and garnish with berries if you desire.
4. Store in the refrigerator and serve at room temperature, garnished with berries, for best flavor.

PER SERVING Net Carbs: 2g | Calories: 345 | Fat: 36g | Carbs: 2g | Protein: 2g | Fiber: 0g

KETO ALMOND BUTTER MOUSSE

This calorie-rich quick snack is like a peanut butter and jelly sandwich in a shot glass. Prepare them early in the week for a midmorning or afternoon snack that's filling and delicious.

PREP TIME 5 MINUTES **YIELD** 6 SHOT GLASSES
SERVING 1 SHOT GLASS

INGREDIENTS

- 1 cup heavy whipping cream
- 4 Tbsp unsalted natural almond butter
- ½ tsp vanilla extract
- 3 drops stevia glycerite
- 18 raspberries
- Mint leaves, for garnish

INSTRUCTIONS

1. Freeze a medium mixing bowl (this will help the cream whip faster) for about 10 minutes. Remove the bowl from the freezer and add the heavy whipping cream, almond butter, vanilla extract and stevia glycerite.
2. Use a hand mixer (or a very strong, patient arm with a whisk) to whip until the batch doubles in size and forms stiff peaks when you pull the mixer away.
3. In a small bowl, muddle 12 raspberries and divide the mixture into the bottom of six shot glasses or three small dessert cups.
4. Spoon the mousse into a pastry bag—or a sandwich bag with the tip cut off—and squeeze on top of the raspberry mixture.
5. Top each with a raspberry and small mint leaf and serve or refrigerate.

PER SERVING Net Carbs: 2g | Calories: 192 | Fat: 19g | Carbs: 4g | Protein: 3g | Fiber: 2g

RED BERRY CHIA JAM

The secret to a keto-friendly jam is chia seeds. They are a natural thickener that turns syrup into jam that you can slather on slices of cheese or Parmesan crackers.

PREP TIME 20 MINUTES **YIELD** 3 CUPS
SERVING 2 TBSP

INGREDIENTS

- 4 cups strawberries or raspberries
- 1 large or 3 small fresh basil leaves
- ¼ cup water
- 1 Tbsp lemon juice
- ¼ cup granulated erythritol
- 15 drops stevia glycerite
- ½ tsp cinnamon
- 2 Tbsp chia seeds

INSTRUCTIONS

1. Remove the stems and roughly chop the strawberries and basil. Leave the strawberries about ½ inch around for a batch with thicker pieces because it pairs better with cheese, but if you're using it for another purpose, cut them as small as you'd like them to appear in your final jam.
2. Over medium heat in a medium saucepan, add the strawberries, basil, water and lemon juice and bring to a simmer.
3. Add the erythritol, stevia glycerite and cinnamon, then mix. Let simmer over medium-low heat for about 10 minutes (the mixture should reduce and thicken).
4. Add the chia seeds, mix and remove from the heat. Let cool for at least 20 minutes. The chia seeds will expand and the mixture will thicken as it cools.
5. Serve or store in an airtight container for up to two weeks.

PER SERVING Net Carbs: 2g | Calories: 23 | Fat: 0g | Carbs: 3g | Protein: 1g | Fiber: 1g

Chilly GARLIC PICKLES

Pickles and pickling spices often have sugar included, so this recipe is for the true keto pickle-lovers—sugar-free and easy to make!

PREP TIME 10 MINUTES **YIELD** 4 CUPS
SERVING ¼ CUP

INGREDIENTS

- 2 lb pickling cucumbers
- 1 ½ cups apple cider vinegar
- 1 ½ cups water
- 2 Tbsp pickling salt
- 6 whole, peeled garlic cloves
- 2 sprigs fresh dill
- 1 tsp whole black peppercorns
- ⅛ tsp mustard seeds

INSTRUCTIONS

1. In a medium saucepan, combine the vinegar, water and pickling salt. Mix to dissolve salt, and once it reaches a boil, remove it from the burner and let cool at least to room temperature.

2. Slice your cucumbers how you'd like them pickled. You can do them tall and long or as ½-inch nuggets.

3. Add the garlic cloves, dill, peppercorns and mustard seeds to the jars or instant pickler, then add sliced cucumbers on top until about ¾ full.

4. Add cooled brine over the pickles, making sure the tops of all the cucumbers are completely covered, but leaving a little room at the top.

5. Cover with the lid and, if using an instant pickler, use the vacuum pump to remove all the air from your pickles, then let them refrigerate for at least 3 hours for half-sour pickles, or overnight for full-sour pickles. If you're doing it the old-fashioned way, you'll want to let them marinate for at least two days.

6. They should last and stay crispy for at least 1 to 2 months in the fridge.

PER SERVING Net Carbs: 0g | Calories: 5 | Fat: 0g | Carbs: 1g | Protein: 0g | Fiber: 2g

BACON AVOCADO DEVILED EGGS

This easy recipe works in some healthy fats from avocados. A little salt and freshly cracked pepper and these bacon avocado deviled eggs are pure gold.

PREP TIME 10 MINUTES **YIELD** 24 EGG HALVES
SERVING 4 EGG HALVES

INGREDIENTS

- 2 slices bacon
- 12 eggs, boiled, shelled
- ½ ripe medium avocado
- Salt and pepper, to taste

INSTRUCTIONS

1. In a skillet, cook the bacon until nice and crispy (you can also use the microwave). Cool, crumble, set aside and reserve ½ teaspoon bacon fat from the pan. Note: You're welcome to make a whole package to gobble at a later date, just reserve about ½ teaspoon of bacon fat. You need bacon fat for the filling or else it will be too dry. You can also use extra virgin olive oil.
2. Slice your eggs in half longways and remove the yolks. In a bowl, combine the yolks from each egg, bacon fat and avocado. Add salt to taste.
3. Organize the egg halves on a plate or serving tray, then spoon or pipe the filling into each egg. Sprinkle with salt, pepper and crumbled bacon.

PER SERVING Net Carbs: 1g | Calories: 110 | Fat: 8g | Carbs: 2g | Protein: 8g | Fiber: 1g

Mains

SOME OF YOUR FAVORITE MEALS ARE SURPRISINGLY KETO-FRIENDLY, AND THE ONES THAT AREN'T ONLY REQUIRE A FEW SIMPLE SUBSTITUTIONS.

DOUBLE-BUTTERED HADDOCK FILLETS

These ultra-buttery haddock fillets are slow-cooked in a rich, buttery lemon broth.

PREP TIME 5 MINUTES **COOK TIME** 2 HOURS ON HIGH **YIELD** 4 FILLETS **SERVING** 1 FILLET **SLOW COOKER SIZE** 6-QUART

INGREDIENTS

- 4 (4-oz) fresh haddock fillets (not frozen, unless defrosted and moisture removed)
- ¾ cup salted butter, melted, divided
- 1 clove garlic, minced
- ½ tsp freshly ground black pepper
- 1 Tbsp lemon juice

GARNISH
- Lemon slices
- Fresh dill

INSTRUCTIONS

1. Place the haddock fillets in the slow cooker, covering the bottom.
2. In a bowl, combine ½ cup melted butter, garlic, pepper and lemon juice, then pour over the fillets.
3. Cook on high for 2 hours, then serve in broth with an extra tablespoon of melted butter over each fillet, a slice of lemon and a few cracks of fresh pepper on top.

PER SERVING Net Carbs: 1g | Calories: 434 | Fat: 36g | Carbs: 1g | Protein: 28g | Fiber: 0g

BEEF & BROCCOLI

Make this classic takeout dish at home to be more in control of the ingredients. Marinated beef is tossed with fresh broccoli and red peppers to complete this craveable feast.

PREP TIME 10 MINUTES **COOK TIME** 6–7 HOURS ON LOW **YIELD** 6 CUPS **SERVING** 1½ CUPS **SLOW COOKER SIZE** 6-QUART

INGREDIENTS

- 2 lb flank steak, sliced into 1–2" chunks
- ⅔ cup liquid coconut aminos or tamari
- 1 cup beef broth
- 10 drops stevia glycerite
- 1 tsp, freshly grated ginger
- 3 garlic cloves, minced
- ½ tsp crushed red pepper flakes (less for mild)
- 1 head broccoli
- 1 red bell pepper
- Salt, pepper and more stevia, to taste

GARNISH

- Sesame seeds
- Scallions, sliced

INSTRUCTIONS

1. Turn the slow cooker to low and add the steak, aminos, beef broth, stevia, ginger, garlic and red pepper flakes.
2. Cook on low for 5 to 6 hours, then stir. Wash and prepare the broccoli and red bell pepper. Chop the broccoli into florets and slice the red bell pepper into large 1-inch pieces. Add to the slow cooker on top of the meat (do not stir) and cook for at least 1 hour, or until they reach your desired doneness. Season with salt, pepper and stevia if you like it sweeter.
3. To thicken your sauce, you can make an arrowroot slurry. Mix 1 tablespoon arrowroot flour with 2 tablespoons cold water (like you would cornstarch) and add to the beef mixture after it's done cooking. If you want it even thicker, repeat until you reach your desired consistency. Arrowroot flour is a common paleo-friendly thickener and it has 1 carb per tablespoon. Xanthan gum also works well.
4. Serve alone or over riced cauliflower (it tastes great with the sauce). Sprinkle with sesame seeds for garnish and serve.

PER SERVING Net Carbs: 3g | Calories: 430 | Fat: 19g | Carbs: 5g | Protein: 54g | Fiber: 2g

PUMPKIN CURRY CHICKEN

Serve this tasty chicken and spicy pumpkin sauce over steamed cauliflower (4 grams net carbs per cup).

PREP TIME 10 MINUTES **COOK TIME** 6–8 HOURS ON LOW **YIELD** 6 CUPS **SERVING** 1 CUP **SLOW COOKER SIZE** 6-QUART

INGREDIENTS

- 1 small pumpkin (about 2 cups cubed or 14-oz can pumpkin)
- 1 (14-oz) can unsweetened coconut milk, cream only
- 2 Tbsp ghee or butter, melted
- 1 Tbsp freshly squeezed lime juice
- ½ small white onion
- 2 Tbsp, chopped fresh Thai basil
- 1 tsp curry powder
- ½ tsp ground coriander
- ½ tsp ground cinnamon
- ½ tsp ground ginger
- ½ tsp sea salt, plus additional for seasoning
- ½ tsp crushed red pepper flakes
- 2 lb boneless chicken breasts
- Cracked black pepper

SERVE OVER
Steamed cauliflower rice or broccoli

INSTRUCTIONS

In a slow cooker, add pumpkin, coconut cream, ghee, lime juice, onion, basil, curry, coriander, cinnamon, ginger, salt, crushed red pepper flakes. Mix, then add the boneless chicken breasts and generously salt and pepper before covering with the sauce. Cook on low for 6 to 8 hours. Serve over steamed cauliflower rice or broccoli.

PER SERVING Net Carbs: 6g | Calories: 363 | Fat: 24g | Carbs: 7g | Protein: 30g | Fiber: 1g

BEEF CARNITAS

Use this spicy shredded beef to stuff roasted peppers or homemade cheddar-cheese taco shells (instructions at right). Since this dish is high in protein, serve with a side that is high in fat.

PREP TIME 10 MINUTES **COOK TIME** 8–10 HOURS ON LOW **YIELD** 6 CUPS **SERVING** ¾ CUP **SLOW COOKER SIZE** 6-QUART

INGREDIENTS

- 1 cup chicken or beef broth
- 1 Tbsp hot sauce
- 3 lb chuck roast
- 2 Tbsp olive oil
- 2 tsp chili powder
- ½ tsp smoked paprika
- 1 tsp cumin
- 1 tsp salt
- ½ tsp freshly ground black pepper
- ½ cup chopped red onion
- 1 Tbsp minced garlic
- 1 (4-oz) can green chilies

GARNISH

- Cilantro
- Lime juice
- Red onions
- Goat cheese
- Avocado, cubed

INSTRUCTIONS

1. Preheat the slow cooker to low and pour in the broth and hot sauce. Rub the roast on all sides with olive oil, then chili powder, paprika, cumin, salt and black pepper, and add the roast to the slow cooker.

2. Top with the onion, garlic and chilies, then cook on low for 8 to 10 hours. Use a fork to shred.

3. For a thicker sauce, add everything to a large skillet and simmer for 10 to 15 minutes until the sauce reduces at least in half.

PER SERVING Net Carbs: 1g | Calories: 435 | Fat: 32g | Carbs: 2g | Protein: 32g | Fiber: 1g

CHINESE RICE & PORK

You probably can't visit a Chinese food restaurant without ogling the pork fried rice on everyone's plates, so why not make it the main course at home? This dish is often made in a pan, but the slow-cooked version allows everything to marinate for better flavor.

PREP TIME 10 MINUTES **COOK TIME** 1–2 HOURS ON HIGH **YIELD** 6 CUPS **SERVING** 1 HEAPING CUP **SLOW COOKER SIZE** 6-QUART

INGREDIENTS

- 4 Tbsp toasted sesame oil
- 2 lb ground pork
- Sea salt
- Freshly ground black pepper
- 3 cups thinly sliced cabbage
- 1 cup chopped broccoli
- 1 red bell pepper, cored, chopped
- 2 cloves garlic, minced
- 1½ cups riced cauliflower
- 2 Tbsp Sriracha sauce
- 4 Tbsp liquid aminos or Tamari
- 2 tsp rice wine vinegar

GARNISH
- Sesame seeds

INSTRUCTIONS

1. Add the sesame seed oil to the skillet over medium-high heat, then add pork and sprinkle generously with salt and pepper. Brown the meat (about 10 minutes), then add to the slow cooker.
2. Add the rest of the ingredients to the slow cooker and mix well. Cook on high for 1 to 2 hours. Add back to the skillet if you want to cook off some of the liquid, then serve.

Tip: Save time by buying the cauliflower pre-riced and using raw coleslaw mix. Don't use frozen veggies, as the mix will get too watery.

PER SERVING Net Carbs: 6g | Calories: 501 | Fat: 39g | Carbs: 9g | Protein: 30g | Fiber: 3g

SAUSAGE STUFFED PEPPERS

Fresh peppers are stuffed with a mix of Italian sausage and riced cauliflower to replicate the easy but delicious family dinners you recognize. And the best part is that most people can't tell the difference!

PREP TIME 15 MINUTES **COOK TIME** 2 HOURS ON HIGH OR 4 HOURS ON LOW **SLOW COOKER SIZE** 6-QUART

INGREDIENTS

- 1 lb ground Italian sausage
- 2 cups riced cauliflower
- ½ tsp salt
- ¼ tsp freshly ground black pepper
- 2 tsp dried Italian seasoning
- 2 cups keto-friendly tomato sauce, divided
- 2 eggs
- 6 medium red, yellow and green bell peppers, tops and cores removed
- 2 cups shredded mozzarella cheese

INSTRUCTIONS

1. In a skillet, brown the Italian sausage. Toss with riced cauliflower, salt, pepper, Italian seasoning and 1½ cups tomato sauce. Turn off the heat, whisk eggs together in a separate bowl and slowly add to mix.

2. Coat the bottom of your slow cooker with the remaining ½ cup tomato sauce, then fill the bell peppers with the mix and add to the bottom of the slow cooker standing up.

3. Cook on high for 2 hours (preferred) or on low for 4 hours. Top with mozzarella cheese and cook until melted, or broil in the oven.

4. Garnish with fresh herbs and serve.

PER SERVING Net Carbs: 7g | Calories: 583 | Fat: 46g | Carbs: 10g | Protein: 36g | Fiber: 3g

PANCETTA CHICKEN BRUSSELS

Pancetta, chicken and Brussels sprouts are paired with a velvety cream sauce that's out of this world. Chicken tenders and breasts are high in protein and low in fat, so the heavy cream helps amp up the fat content in this dish.

PREP TIME 10 MINUTES **COOK TIME** 2–3 HOURS ON HIGH OR 4–5 HOURS ON LOW **YIELD** 6 CUPS **SERVING** 1 HEAPING CUP **SLOW COOKER SIZE** 6-QUART

INGREDIENTS

- 3 lb chicken tenderloins
- 3 cups trimmed Brussels sprouts
- 1 tsp minced garlic
- 4 oz thick pancetta, cut into ½" pieces
- 1 lemon, quartered, deseeded
- 1 cup chicken broth
- 1 cup heavy cream

INSTRUCTIONS

1. In a slow cooker, add the chicken tenderloins, Brussels sprouts, minced garlic and pancetta, and lay the lemon slices over the top.
2. Cook on high for 2 to 3 hours or on low for 4 to 5 hours.
3. When ready, toss everything together, then drain excess liquid from the bottom and remove the lemons.
4. To make the cream sauce, simply add the chicken broth to a skillet over medium-high heat until it reduces in half (5 to 10 minutes), then add the heavy cream until it reduces in half again. Pour in the slow cooker and toss, then serve.

PER SERVING Net Carbs: 5g | Calories: 436 | Fat: 23g | Carbs: 7g | Protein: 55g | Fiber: 2g

Cheesy BARBECUE MONTEREY CHICKEN

This dish can be cooked entirely in the slow cooker, or finished in the oven or even on the grill. You can also buy a keto-friendly barbecue sauce or make your own (directions at right). Serve with an oil-dressed salad or some buttery veggies to add more fat to this meal.

PREP TIME 10 MINUTES **COOK TIME** 2–3 HOURS ON HIGH OR 4–5 HOURS ON LOW **YIELD** 6 THIGHS **SERVING** 1 THIGH **SLOW COOKER SIZE** 6-QUART

INGREDIENTS
- Salt and pepper
- 6 chicken thighs, boneless, skinless
- 1 cup sugar-free, keto-friendly barbecue sauce, divided
- 1 cup shredded cheddar cheese
- ½ cup crumbled bacon, precooked

GARNISH
- Scallions
- Tomatoes, finely chopped

INSTRUCTIONS
1. Generously salt and pepper the chicken thighs, then add ½ cup barbecue sauce to the slow cooker and add thighs. Drizzle some of the sauce over the chicken, then cook on low for 4 to 5 hours (preferred) or on high for 2 to 3 hours.

2. Remove the chicken from the slow cooker and drain. Add the chicken back in, dollop each thigh with the remaining barbecue sauce, then add the cheddar cheese, bacon crumbles and cover, continuing to cook until the cheese is melted (about 15 minutes). If you have a removable crock and want quicker results, put the crock in the oven and broil until the cheese melts and gets crispy.

3. Garnish with scallions, chopped tomatoes and freshly ground black pepper, if desired.

PER SERVING Net Carbs: 2g | Calories: 313 | Fat: 19g | Carbs: 3g | Protein: 31g | Fiber: 1g

SPINACH & ARTICHOKE CHICKEN

If you love classic spinach and artichoke dip, get ready to fall in love with this creamy chicken dish that uses all of the same flavors.

PREP TIME 5 MINUTES **COOK TIME** 2–3 HOURS ON HIGH OR 5–6 HOURS ON LOW **YIELD** 6 CUPS **SERVING** 1 CUP **SLOW COOKER SIZE** 6-QUART

INGREDIENTS

- 4 handfuls fresh spinach (about 5 oz)
- 8.5 oz quartered artichoke hearts, drained
- 2-3 lb chicken thighs, boneless, skinless
- 1 tsp garlic powder
- ½ tsp salt
- ½ tsp freshly ground black pepper
- 16 oz cream cheese, sliced or cubed
- ¼ cup mayonnaise
- 1 cup shredded mozzarella
- 1 red bell pepper, destemmed, chopped

INSTRUCTIONS

1. In a slow cooker, add spinach and artichokes, then chicken thighs. Season with garlic powder, salt and pepper. Top with the sliced or cubed cream cheese.

2. Cook for 2 to 3 hours on high (preferred) or 5 to 6 hours on low. The chicken should be easily shredded with a fork. It will be a little watery at this point. Mix, then add the mayonnaise, mozzarella and red bell pepper and mix, then let cook another 15 minutes before serving.

PER SERVING Net Carbs: 6g | Calories: 594 | Fat: 45g | Carbs: 8g | Protein: 35g | Fiber: 2g

BUTTER CHICKEN

This meal can be made in a pinch with ingredients most of us have in our cupboards. Garam masala is the more authentic approach to traditional Indian butter chicken that includes cinnamon, cloves and cardamom for ubiquitous Indian flavor, but it requires a lot of ingredients, many with added carbohydrates. This version uses curry powder instead for a unique flavor with a silky, rich tomato sauce.

PREP TIME 10 MINUTES **COOK TIME** 4 HOURS ON HIGH OR 8–10 HOURS ON LOW **YIELD** 8 CUPS **SERVING** 1 CUP **SLOW COOKER SIZE** 6-QUART

INGREDIENTS

- 28 oz crushed tomatoes
- 6 Tbsp butter or ghee, divided
- ½ medium yellow onion, finely diced
- 2 Tbsp curry powder
- 8 chicken thighs, skinless, boneless
- Salt and pepper
- ¾ cup heavy cream

OPTIONAL: Serve atop steamed cauliflower rice (3g extra net carbs per cup)

GARNISH
Cilantro, chopped

INSTRUCTIONS

1. Add the crushed tomatoes to the slow cooker. To get the most flavor out of this dish, heat a medium skillet to medium-low and melt 2 tablespoons ghee or butter. Then add in the onion and curry powder, cooking just a couple minutes until the curry toasts and is fragrant. Add the onions into the tomato sauce.

2. Generously season the chicken thighs with salt and pepper on both sides. Sear the chicken thighs 1 minute on each side, then add to the slow cooker and cover with sauce. (In a rush? Skip the above steps, and add all of the above directly into the slow cooker.)

3. Cook on low for 8 to 10 hours or on high for 4 hours, then add the heavy cream and remaining 4 tablespoons butter right before serving, then mix. Use a spoon to break up the chicken gently into the sauce and, if desired, serve atop steamed riced cauliflower and garnish generously with cilantro.

PER SERVING Net Carbs: 5g | Calories: 312 | Fat: 24g | Carbs: 7g | Protein: 20g | Fiber: 2g

Cheesy TACO BEEF

While a lot of the cooking for this recipe happens in the pan, the slow cooker marinates the beef to perfection. This spicy taco beef is perfect for serving a crowd or for meal prep. If you're avoiding dairy, simply skip the cheese at the end.

PREP TIME 10 MINUTES **COOK TIME** 3–4 HOURS ON HIGH OR 6–8 HOURS ON LOW **YIELD** 6 CUPS **SERVING** 1 CUP **SLOW COOKER SIZE** 6-QUART

INGREDIENTS

- 1 Tbsp olive or avocado oil
- 2 lb ground beef
- 1 (4-oz) can green chilies
- 4 Tbsp chili powder
- 2 Tbsp cumin
- ½ Tbsp smoked paprika
- 1 Tbsp salt
- 1 tsp garlic powder
- 1 tsp onion powder
- ½ tsp whole oregano
- 1 tsp freshly ground black pepper
- ¼ tsp red pepper flakes
- ⅛ tsp cayenne pepper
- 10 drops stevia glycerite
- 1 Tbsp tomato paste
- ¼ tsp xanthan gum or arrowroot powder
- 1 cup shredded cheddar cheese
- ½ Tbsp orange zest (optional)

INSTRUCTIONS

1. In a skillet over medium heat, brown the ground beef, then add it to the slow cooker.
2. Add the can of green chilies, all of the spices, stevia, tomato paste and xanthan gum and mix. Cook on low for 6 to 8 hours (preferred) or on high for 3 to 4 hours. Add cheddar cheese and mix, then let melt before serving.

PER SERVING Net Carbs: 3g | Calories: 445 | Fat: 32g | Carbs: 6g | Protein: 36g | Fiber: 3g

CHICKEN CACCIATORE

This dairy-free keto staple is full of flavors, incorporating many of your favorite low-carb vegetables into a comforting chicken dinner with an addictively delicious, spicy red sauce.

PREP TIME 15 MINUTES **COOK TIME** 4 HOURS ON HIGH OR 8 HOURS ON LOW **YIELD** 9 CUPS **SERVING** 1½ CUPS **SLOW COOKER SIZE** 6-QUART

INGREDIENTS

- 1 (28-oz) can diced tomatoes
- 1 medium yellow onion, chopped
- 1 red bell pepper, seeded, sliced into strips
- 1 green bell pepper, seeded, sliced into strips
- 1 Tbsp minced garlic
- 2 tsp oregano
- 1 tsp basil
- 2 tsp red pepper flakes
- 1 cup sliced white mushrooms
- 8 chicken thighs, boneless, skinless
- 4 Tbsp olive oil
- ½ cup red wine
- 1½ cups tomato sauce (no sugar added)
- ½ Tbsp salt
- ½ Tbsp coarse black pepper

GARNISH

- Fresh parsley
- Parmesan, grated (optional)

INSTRUCTIONS

1. In a slow cooker, add the diced tomatoes, onion, bell peppers, garlic, oregano, basil, red pepper flakes and mushrooms and preheat to low.

2. Add chicken thighs to slow cooker or, for a more robust traditional flavor, sear first using this method: In a skillet, heat 2 tablespoons olive oil over medium-high, then sear the thighs for about 4 minutes on each side in two batches (adding 2 tablespoons of olive oil between batches). Add to the slow cooker, then over high heat, add red wine to the pan and use a spatula to scrape the pan for about 2 minutes while the alcohol cooks off, and the result is a savory wine stock that will flavor your sauce. Add it all into the slow cooker.

3. Cook on high for 4 hours or on low for 8 hours.

4. Add tomato sauce, salt and pepper and mix. Add more red pepper flakes to taste, if you want more of a kick. Use a spoon to mix, and gently break up the chicken into the sauce leaving large chunks, careful not to shred too much. Serve in a bowl or over zoodles.

PER SERVING Net Carbs: 6g | Calories: 461 | Fat: 36g | Carbs: 8g | Protein: 25g | Fiber: 2g
(Note: These nutrition facts assume all sauce is consumed.)

GREEK CHICKEN
in Lemon Egg Sauce

A creamy lemon sauce doesn't need flour when it uses tempered eggs to thicken. And a velvety sauce that uses fresh lemon juice is perfect for this Greek-seasoned chicken.

PREP TIME 15 MINUTES **COOK TIME** 4 HOURS ON HIGH OR 6–8 HOURS ON LOW **YIELD** 4 SERVINGS **SERVING** 2 THIGHS WITH SAUCE **SLOW COOKER SIZE** 6-QUART

INGREDIENTS

- 2 cups, plus ¼ cup chicken broth
- 1 large lemon (juice and zest)
- 6 Tbsp unsalted butter, sliced
- 1 Tbsp oregano
- 1 tsp minced garlic
- 1 tsp salt
- 1 tsp freshly ground black pepper
- 8 small chicken thighs, bone-in, skin-on
- 2 large eggs

GARNISH

- Fresh oregano
- Freshly cracked pepper

INSTRUCTIONS

1. In a slow cooker, add 2 cups chicken broth, lemon juice and zest, butter, oregano, garlic, salt and pepper.

2. Season the chicken generously with salt and pepper, add 2 tablespoons oil to a large skillet and sear skin-side down. Cook in two batches if necessary, adding 2 additional tablespoons when you do the second batch. The skins are done when they're crisp and don't stick to the pan. Add to the slow cooker as they're done, skin-side up—do not cover with broth so the skin stays crispy.

3. When all pieces are seared, add ¼ cup chicken broth to the skillet while still hot and use a spatula to scrape the burned bits off the pan. Add the bits and the broth into the slow cooker. (Tip: If you want to skip this step for the sake of time, use boneless, skinless chicken thighs instead and add directly to the slow cooker.)

4. Cook on high for 4 hours or on low for 6 to 8 hours.

5. When the chicken is cooked, turn off the slow cooker and plate the chicken. Add two large eggs into a bowl and whisk or beat until smooth. Use a ladle to slowly drip the sauce into the bowl while you whisk. This is called "tempering" and it is used to bring the eggs up to temperature so they don't scramble when you add them to the slow cooker. Once hot, add to the slow cooker and whisk again to thicken the sauce, then use the ladle to pour over the chicken immediately.

PER SERVING Net Carbs: 1g | Calories: 730 | Fat: 56g | Carbs: 1g | Protein: 54g | Fiber: 0g

ITALIAN CHICKEN LASAGNA

It's true that veggie noodles don't hold up well to a slow cooker, but thinly sliced chicken is a perfect substitute. Paired with savory sausage, you won't believe how much this recipe tastes like the real thing. If you choose to omit the veggies (peppers and onions), you'll save 2.5 grams of carbs per serving.

PREP TIME 15 MINUTES **COOK TIME** 2 HOURS ON HIGH **YIELD** 12 SLICES **SERVING** 1 SLICE **SLOW COOKER SIZE** 6-QUART

INGREDIENTS

- 1 lb ground Italian sausage
- 3 cups keto-friendly tomato sauce, divided
- 1 cup finely diced red onion
- 1 cup finely diced red bell pepper
- 1 cup finely diced green bell pepper
- 2 cloves garlic, minced
- 15 oz whole milk ricotta cheese
- 2 large eggs
- 1 Tbsp chopped fresh basil
- ⅛ tsp salt and pinch of pepper
- 18 deli chicken breast slices
- 2 cups shredded mozzarella cheese

GARNISH
Fresh basil and parsley, chopped
Parmesan, grated or shredded

INSTRUCTIONS

1. Brown the ground sausage in a skillet over medium heat. Remove, leaving 1 tablespoon grease in the pan, and toss the sausage with 2½ cups tomato sauce.
2. Add the onions, peppers and garlic to the pan and cook until softened and moisture has cooked off. Note: This step can be skipped and vegetables can be added raw, however your lasagna may have a little liquid in the bottom when it's done cooking.
3. In one bowl, whisk your ricotta cheese and eggs together until smooth, then add basil, salt and pepper and mix.
4. Grease your slow cooker, then add the remaining ½ cup tomato sauce to the bottom. Top with six slices of chicken. Split the rest of the ingredients in thirds for three layers and top the chicken in this order: chicken, ricotta mix, pepper mix, mozzarella, tomato sauce. Do this for two more layers, but swap the sauce and mozzarella in the top later so the mozzarella is the final top layer.
5. Cook on high for 2 hours, then cut into slices.

PER SERVING Net Carbs: 7g | Calories: 374 | Fat: 27g | Carbs: 8g | Protein: 24g | Fiber: 1g

WHOLE BUTTER & HERB CHICKEN

Have you ever tried cooking a whole chicken in your slow cooker? As you can imagine, the meat falls right off the bone. Plus, the leftovers make a great start to chicken bone broth, so win-win! If you're avoiding dairy, use ghee instead of butter.

PREP TIME 10 MINUTES **COOK TIME** 4–5 HOURS ON LOW OR 8 HOURS ON LOW **YIELD** 8 CUPS CHICKEN MEAT **SERVING** 1 CUP **SLOW COOKER SIZE** 6-QUART

INGREDIENTS

- 5 lb organic chicken
- 1 cup salted butter, softened
- 2 Tbsp Herbes de Provence
- 1 lemon, sliced, deseeded
- ½ tsp garlic powder
- Salt and pepper

INSTRUCTIONS

1. Use a slow cooker roasting rack or simply use twisted or balled up foil to keep your bird lifted off the bottom so it doesn't get soggy.
2. Slide your fingers under the skin of your chicken, starting near the cavern and leading toward the neck. Try to create a pocket without tearing the skin.
3. Combine softened butter and herbes de Provence in a bowl and cream together. Rub butter mixture all over the chicken and under the skin.
4. Place lemon slices in the cavern of the chicken—along with anything else you'd like to add for aroma, like onions or rosemary. Sprinkle the bird with the garlic powder, salt and pepper. Tie the legs together with cooking twine.
5. Cook on high for 4 to 5 hours or on high for 1 hour, then low for 8 hours (this is for food safety). The chicken is ready when it's at least 165 degrees F when you check the thighs.
6. Transfer your bird from the slow cooker to the oven in a cast iron skillet and broil for 5 to 10 minutes until crispy.

PER SERVING Net Carbs: 0g | Calories: 728 | Fat: 61g | Carbs: 0g | Protein: 48g | Fiber: 0g

GARLIC BUTTER POT ROAST

If you're looking for a juicy, tender pot roast, chuck roast provides the most tender meat that will fall apart when ready. For best results, cook low and slow for fork-tender bites.

PREP TIME 10 MINUTES **COOK TIME** 8 HOURS ON LOW
YIELD 10 CUPS WITH GRAVY **SERVING** 1 CUP
SLOW COOKER SIZE 6-QUART

INGREDIENTS

- 1½ Tbsp onion powder
- 3 Tbsp chopped fresh parsley, or 1½ Tbsp dried parsley
- 2 Tbsp chopped fresh oregano, or 1 Tbsp dried oregano
- 2 tsp fresh thyme leaves, or ¼ tsp dried thyme
- 1 Tbsp sea salt or garlic salt
- 2 tsp dried dill weed
- 2 tsp garlic powder
- 2 tsp freshly ground black pepper
- ¼ tsp celery salt
- 3 lb chuck roast
- 2 Tbsp olive oil
- 2 cups beef or chicken broth
- 1 Tbsp Worcestershire sauce
- 8 garlic cloves
- 6 Tbsp ghee or butter

INSTRUCTIONS

1. In a bowl, combine all of the fresh and dried herbs, salts and pepper, then rub the mixture all over the chuck roast.

2. In a medium skillet over medium heat, add olive oil and, once hot, sear all sides of the chuck roast. Add to the slow cooker, then pour in the broth and Worcestershire sauce and add the garlic cloves.

3. Set your slow cooker to low for at least 8 hours. Check to make sure it's fork-tender before you serve. When ready, add ghee to the drippings. Serve alongside your favorite vegetables.

Optional: To thicken drippings into a gravy, add ¼ teaspoon xanthan gum at a time with a whisk until it reaches your desired consistency.

PER SERVING Net Carbs: 2g | Calories: 680 | Fat: 49g | Carbs: 2g | Protein: 58g | Fiber: 0g

Sweet & Smoky
BARBECUE PULLED PORK

It only takes a few minutes in the morning to have a plate of pulled pork ready for dinner. Pair this dish with a buttery side, or top a plate of keto nachos with all the fixings!

PREP TIME 5 MINUTES **COOK TIME** 8–10 HOURS ON LOW **YIELD** 8 CUPS **SERVING** 1 CUP **SLOW COOKER SIZE** 6-QUART

INGREDIENTS
- 2½ lb pork shoulder/butt, fat trimmed
- ¼ tsp salt
- ¼ tsp freshly ground black pepper
- ½ cup apple cider vinegar
- 1 (15-oz) can tomato sauce
- ⅔ cup keto-friendly brown sugar (e.g. Lakanto® or Swerve®)
- 1 Tbsp Worcestershire sauce
- 5 drops liquid smoke
- 1 tsp smoked paprika
- ½ tsp cayenne pepper
- ¼ tsp garlic powder
- ¼ tsp onion powder

INSTRUCTIONS
1. Rub the pork with a generous amount of salt and pepper. (For a spicier pulled pork, rub with 1 teaspoon chili powder too.) Add the pork to the slow cooker and cook low and slow for 8 to 10 hours. It will create its own juices, though some people prefer a few tablespoons of apple cider vinegar in the bottom.
2. When the pork is about done, add the rest of the ingredients to a saucepan over medium heat. Taste and adjust to your specific preferences. You can also add hot mustard for more of a Carolina zing. Cook for about 10 minutes, or until hot.
3. When the pork is done, remove any excess fat and liquid, then tear apart with a fork. Add the sauce to the slow cooker, mix and serve.

PER SERVING Net Carbs: 3g | Calories: 353 | Fat: 26g | Carbs: 4g | Protein: 25g | Fiber: 1g

PHILLY CHEESE STEAK STUFFED PEPPERS

Easily made ahead and even better reheated, these stuffed peppers hit every branch on their way down the "taste" tree.

PREP TIME 30 MINUTES **YIELD** 4 STUFFED PEPPERS
SERVING 1 STUFFED PEPPER

INGREDIENTS

- 4 green peppers
- 3 Tbsp extra-virgin olive oil
- ¼ cup chopped onions
- 1 tsp minced garlic
- 1 lb shaved beef steak
- 2 Tbsp mayonnaise
- 1 Tbsp Dijon mustard
- 5 slices pepper jack cheese

INSTRUCTIONS

1. Preheat oven to 400 degrees F. Cut the tops off the green peppers and place them in the oven on a baking sheet to cook for about 10 minutes. Cut around the stem of the green pepper tops (discard those) and chop up the extra green pepper that's left.

2. In a medium skillet over medium heat, add the olive oil and, once melted, add the onions, green peppers and garlic, cooking for about 2 minutes.

3. Add the shaved steak to the pan, then generously salt and pepper the meat. Brown the meat until fully cooked, chopping with your spatula as you go. Add one slice of cheese and mix until melted. Remove from heat and toss with the mayonnaise and Dijon mustard.

4. Take the green peppers out of the oven when they're soft but not too soft to stuff. There should be some juice in the bottom of the shells—don't dump it, it adds flavor!

5. Spoon the steak mixture into the green pepper shells, then top each with a slice of cheese. Add back into the oven to broil for 3 to 5 minutes, or until the cheese is melted to your liking, then serve hot.

6. Serve in bowls with slices of avocado and dollops of sour cream. Optionally, you can also garnish with chopped scallions and jalapeños.

PER SERVING Net Carbs: 4g | Calories: 514 | Fat: 39g | Carbs: 6g | Protein: 29g | Fiber: 2g

5-Minute UPSIDE DOWN PIZZA

In 5 minutes, you can have a keto-friendly meal that is super-filling and tastes like our favorite comfort food: pizza! Fried mozzarella cheese is on the bottom instead of the top, as a perfect stand-in for the crust.

PREP TIME 5 MINUTES **YIELD** 1 PIZZA **SERVING** 1

INGREDIENTS

- 1 Tbsp extra-virgin olive oil
- 1 cup shredded whole-milk mozzarella cheese
- 4 Tbsp shredded Asiago cheese
- 1 tsp Italian seasoning
- 1 tsp garlic powder
- ⅓ cup no-sugar-added marinara sauce, heated
- 1 Tbsp grated Parmesan
- Fresh basil (optional)

INSTRUCTIONS

1. Over medium heat in a small nonstick pan (a 6-inch egg pan works well), heat up the olive oil and roll around the pan, being sure to cover the whole bottom.

2. Once hot, add the mozzarella and Asiago cheese and use a spatula to round all the edges and keep a uniform shape. Sprinkle with Italian seasoning and garlic powder to flavor the "crust."

3. Cook for about 3 to 5 minutes until it melts and starts to become dark around the edges. Use a spatula to test doneness by sliding it under the crust, starting from the edges. If the cheese is still melty in the middle, keep cooking until crisp all the way around.

4. When ready, the crust should easily slide out onto a plate. Let cool for 1 minute to harden, then top with the warmed tomato sauce and use a spoon to spread, then top with the grated Parmesan and basil, if desired. Cut into quarters and serve.

PER SERVING Net Carbs: 5g | Calories: 603 | Fat: 51g | Carbs: 5g | Protein: 30g | Fiber: 0g

CHILI CASSEROLE

This casserole uses finely chopped cauliflower as a rice-like base that even the pickiest eaters enjoy when it's saturated with thick, meaty chili.

PREP TIME 45 MINUTES **YIELD** 8 CUPS **SERVING** 1 CUP

INGREDIENTS

- 3 cups fresh cauliflower, finely chopped into ¼" pieces
- 2 Tbsp olive oil
- 2 lb ground beef
- 2 Tbsp chili powder
- 1 Tbsp smoked paprika
- 1 Tbsp cumin
- 1 tsp onion powder
- 1 tsp cinnamon
- 1 tsp sea salt
- 1 tsp minced garlic
- ½ tsp cayenne pepper
- ½ Tbsp oregano
- 2 (10-oz) cans diced tomatoes with chilies
- 1 cup shredded cheddar cheese
- 1 cup sour cream
- 1 ripe avocado

GARNISH (OPTIONAL)
- Jalapeño
- Scallions

INSTRUCTIONS

1. Preheat oven to 350 degrees F and grease a 2-quart, 9-by-9-inch casserole dish.

2. Cover the bottom with the chopped cauliflower; the pieces should be chopped small by hand, about ¼-inch pieces.

3. In a medium skillet over medium heat, heat the olive oil, then cook the beef for about 10 minutes until browned, then add chili seasonings (chili powder, smoked paprika, cumin, onion powder, cinnamon, salt, minced garlic, cayenne pepper, oregano), along with diced tomatoes and mix, then let simmer for 5 minutes to cook off some of the excess moisture.

4. Pour the meat mixture over the chopped cauliflower and use a spatula to press down so the juices penetrate through the cauliflower layer.

5. Bake for 30 minutes, wrapped in tinfoil or otherwise covered. Uncover and top with shredded cheddar cheese, then bake for an additional 5 to 10 minutes uncovered until the cheese melts and begins to brown and bubble.

6. Serve in bowls with slices of avocado and dollops of sour cream. You can also garnish with chopped scallions and jalapeños.

PER SERVING Net Carbs: 7g | Calories: 507 | Fat: 38g | Carbs: 11g | Protein: 29g | Fiber: 4g

Easy CHICKEN PARM AND ZOODLES

For an easy weeknight meal, this spin on classic chicken Parmesan uses crushed pork rinds for the breading and a roaster rack to keep the chicken crispy. They taste perfect on top of some lightly sautéed zucchini noodles.

PREP TIME 60 MINUTES **YIELD** 4 SERVINGS **SERVING** 1

INGREDIENTS

- 2 (4-oz) chicken breasts (pounded and tenderized until flat)
- 3 Tbsp olive oil (divided)
- 2 cups crushed pork rinds
- ½ cup grated Parmesan
- 2 Tbsp Italian seasoning
- 1 cup shredded whole-milk mozzarella cheese
- 4 small or medium zucchini
- 1 tsp garlic salt
- 1 cup naturally low-carb tomato sauce (6g per cup or less)
- Salt and pepper

INSTRUCTIONS

1. Preheat oven to 375 degrees F.

2. Place your chicken breasts between two slices of plastic wrap and pound until flat. Divide into four total pieces and rub with 1 tablespoon olive oil, then sprinkle with salt and pepper. In a plastic bag or container, combine the pork rinds, Parmesan cheese and Italian seasoning. Add your four chicken breast halves to the bag and shake them up until totally covered.

3. Place your coated chicken breasts on a roaster rack over a baking sheet and generously salt and pepper them. The roasting rack will allow the breasts to crisp all the way around.

4. Sprinkle about ½ cup mozzarella cheese on each chicken breast and cook for 30 to 45 minutes, or until they reach 180 degrees F.

5. Meanwhile, use a zoodler to create zucchini noodles with your four zucchini. If you don't have a zoodler, you can use a vegetable peeler to make "ribbons" that will resemble fettuccini but will produce less than a zoodler. Discard the centers. Add garlic salt to zoodles and toss. Let sit until they're ready to be cooked, then use a paper towel to dry the zoodles, as the salt will have drawn out extra moisture you want to remove.

6. Add the zoodles to pan and let cook for 1 to 2 minutes, just enough to get them hot or they'll become soggy.

7. Add the tomato sauce and cook only until hot, then use a fork or tong to plate your zoodles with your chicken. Drizzle any remaining tomato sauce from the pan over your chicken along with the remaining mozzarella cheese. Serve.

PER SERVING Net Carbs: 4g | Calories: 546 | Fat: 38g | Carbs: 5g | Protein: 48g | Fiber: 1g

SHEET PAN SAUSAGE AND PEPPERS
with Mustard Dressing

Feel like you're at the ballpark with this easy ketogenic meal made with Italian sausage and savory peppers tossed in a mustard dressing.

PREP TIME 25 MINUTES **YIELD** 4 SERVINGS
SERVING 2 SAUSAGES AND ½ CUP PEPPERS AND ONIONS

INGREDIENTS
- ½ yellow onion
- ½ red bell pepper
- ½ green bell pepper
- ½ yellow bell pepper
- 2½ Tbsp olive oil, divided
- Salt and pepper
- 8 Italian sausages in casings
- ½ Tbsp yellow mustard
- ⅛ tsp apple cider vinegar

INSTRUCTIONS
1. Preheat oven to 400 degrees F.
2. Slice the onions and peppers into long strips and arrange them on a small sheet pan, and toss with 2 tablespoons olive oil, salt and pepper. Place the Italian sausages on top of the peppers and bake for 20 minutes, shuffling about halfway through so the vegetables don't burn.
3. Meanwhile, make the dressing by mixing the mustard, apple cider vinegar and ½ tablespoon olive oil.
4. When done baking, drizzle with the mustard dressing, toss and serve.

PER SERVING Net Carbs: 4g | Calories: 307 | Fat: 25g | Carbs: 5g | Protein: 14g | Fiber: 1g

CHICKEN BACON RANCH TACO

The real benefit of this recipe is learning how to make taco shells made of bacon! A great flavor combination is chicken, ranch and bacon, but feel free to fill them with your favorite fixings.

PREP TIME 10 MINUTES **YIELD** 1 TACO **SERVING** 1 TACO

INGREDIENTS

- 5 strips bacon
- ¼ cup grilled chicken
- 2 Tbsp ranch dressing
- 1 romaine leaf
-   Pinch of cracked black pepper
- ⅛ tsp freshly chopped chives

INSTRUCTIONS

1. Find a large microwave-safe bowl and hang five full bacon strips along the side, slightly overlapping them so they cook together. Alternatively, you can use an oven and bake them over an oven-safe glass dish at 400 degrees F for 15 minutes.

2. In the microwave, cook for about 4 minutes on high, then check on the bacon. If you want to get them crispier, keep cooking in 30-second intervals.

3. Once cooked, remove the bowl and bacon, and let them hang until they're hardened into their shell shape. The longer you cook them, the harder the shell will be. Trim them with kitchen shears to create an authentic taco shell shape, if you desire.

4. In a small skillet, over medium heat, toss the chicken with ranch dressing. (It can also be served cold.) Fill the shell with the lettuce leaf for extra reinforcement, then the chicken, and top with pepper and freshly chopped chives.

PER SERVING Net Carbs: 3g | Calories: 342 | Fat: 33g | Carbs: 3g | Protein: 11g | Fiber: 0g

BUFFALO CHICKEN DIVAN

This recipe spices up traditional chicken divan, which uses canned soup, transforming it into a creamier version using cream cheese. Rotisserie chicken is shredded for faster prep time, but you can also bake and shred two large chicken breasts.

PREP TIME 40 MINUTES **YIELD** 6 SLICES
SERVING 1 SLICE

INGREDIENTS

- 1 cup hot sauce
- ½ cup unsalted butter
- 1 tsp smoked paprika
- 1 tsp garlic powder
- ½ tsp salt
- 4 cups shredded rotisserie chicken
- 8 oz cream cheese, cubed
- 1 cup blue cheese dressing
- 2 cups broccoli, chopped (bite size)
- 2 cups cheddar cheese, divided

INSTRUCTIONS

1. Preheat oven to 350 degrees F and grease a 9-by-9-inch baking dish.
2. In a medium saucepan, heat the sauce, butter and spices until melted, then add the chicken and cook until hot.
3. Add the cubed cream cheese and mix until melted, then add the blue cheese dressing and remove from heat.
4. Toss with the broccoli and 1 cup cheddar, transfer to baking dish and bake for 20 minutes. Add the remaining cup of cheddar cheese to the top and bake another 10 minutes. Cool and serve.

PER SERVING Net Carbs: 5g | Calories: 689 | Fat: 64g | Carbs: 6 | Protein: 25g | Fiber: 1g

MEXICAN SKILLET PIZZA

The best part about Mexican pizza is you can top it with all your favorite taco ingredients since they're all fresh, and many are naturally low-carb and high-fat, like sour cream and avocado.

PREP TIME 10 MINUTES **YIELD** 1 PIZZA
SERVING 1 PIZZA

INGREDIENTS

- ½ lb grass-fed ground beef
- ¼ cup water
- 1 tsp chili powder
- ½ tsp smoked paprika
- ½ tsp ground cumin
- ½ tsp salt
- ½ tsp freshly ground black pepper
- ¼ tsp onion powder

CRUST

- 2 Tbsp olive oil
- ½ cup four-cheese Mexican blend (this blend will keep it from sticking to the pan)
- 3/4 cup shredded cheddar cheese

Pizza topping options: Salsa, pico de gallo, shredded lettuce, shredded cheddar, sour cream, avocado, hot sauce, sliced jalapeño, cilantro

INSTRUCTIONS

1. In a small skillet over medium-high heat, brown the ground beef. Add ¼ cup water and dry taco meat ingredients, then simmer on low for 5 to 10 minutes until reduced.
2. In the meantime, heat a medium skillet to medium heat and add 2 tablespoons olive oil.
3. Once hot, very quickly add the Mexican blend first to the pan, then the cheddar on top, then use a silicone spatula to form the edges into a circle.
4. Cook for about 4 to 5 minutes until the cheese easily lifts with a spatula. Use the spatula to lift the edges of the pizza from the pan, going around the edges first and then the middle, until the whole crust can easily slide out (if it doesn't, keep cooking).
5. Tip your skillet to slide your pizza onto a plate. Top with your favorite seasonings, starting with your taco meat and any salsa on the bottom layer. Example: Salsa, then taco meat, shredded lettuce, pico de gallo, shredded cheddar cheese, dollops of sour cream and guacamole, then shake some hot sauce over the top.
6. Cut into quarters and serve.

PER SERVING Net Carbs: 2g | Calories: 948 | Fat: 72g | Carbs: 2g | Protein: 70g | Fiber: 0g

CURRY BUTTER BALLS

These butter balls, flavored with traditional Indian spices, lends perfectly to a low-carb, high-fat diet because it embraces a healthy dose of fats by design. Serve alone or with riced cauliflower, which will taste amazing soaking up the extra sauce.

PREP TIME 10 MINUTES **YIELD** 40 MEATBALLS
SERVING 5 MEATBALLS

INGREDIENTS

- 2 lb ground chicken
- 3 large eggs
- ½ cup coconut flour
- ½ Tbsp ground turmeric
- ½ Tbsp ground cinnamon
- ½ Tbsp salt
- ½ Tbsp lemon juice

OPTIONAL: Prepared and steamed cauliflower rice to serve with
GARNISH: De-stemmed and chopped cilantro

SAUCE

- 1 cup diced white onion (about ¾ onion)
- 5 Tbsp ghee
- 1 Tbsp minced garlic
- 1 Tbsp freshly grated ginger
- 1 tsp curry powder
- 2 tsp salt
- 28 oz crushed tomatoes
- 2 Tbsp garam masala
- 1 Tbsp ground cumin
- 1½ cups heavy cream

INSTRUCTIONS

1. Preheat oven to 400 degrees F, then line two large baking sheets with parchment paper.
2. In a large bowl, combine the ground chicken, eggs, coconut flour, turmeric, cinnamon, salt and lemon juice. Use your hands to mix the ingredients well.
3. Form the mixture into about 40 meatballs about 1½ to 2 inches thick, placing them on the large baking sheet. Note: Ground chicken is sticky, and while the coconut flour helps, try adding olive oil to your hands before making the balls to help them roll smoother. Another trick is to keep a bowl of cold water next to you, dipping your hands often before making the meatballs. If they're not perfect, don't worry. You can flip them throughout the cooking cycle to keep them from getting crispy peaks.
4. Bake until the internal temperature reaches 165 degrees F, about 15 to 20 minutes then remove from the oven. While cooking, roll the meatballs a few times so they end up smooth and round.
5. While the balls are baking, begin making your sauce. In a small saucepan, melt the ghee and cook the onion over medium-low heat for 3 minutes until tender, being careful not to burn.
6. Add garlic, ginger, curry powder and salt and cook an extra minute, then add the tomatoes and let simmer for 10 to 15 minutes until thicker. Add the heavy cream and bring to a simmer. Taste and add salt and pepper as needed. If you want more spice, add more curry ½ teaspoon at a time.
7. Add the meatballs to the sauce and let marinate over low heat at least 10 minutes. Serve alone or over hot steamed cauliflower rice. Garnish with cilantro.

PER SERVING Net Carbs: 9g | Calories: 651 | Fat: 44g | Carbs: 17g | Protein: 47g | Fiber: 8g
(Note: Nutrition data includes sauce. Subtract 5 net carbs if you skip extra sauce with your meatballs.)

Candied GARLIC CHICKEN THIGHS

This dish will make you look like the cast-iron-slinging superhero of keto dinner, and it only takes a few flicks of your arm to put together. These chicken thighs, sprinkled with lemon and sizzled with rosemary, will crisp right up in the oven while whole cloves of garlic caramelize. Tip: Frozen garlic cloves keep them from burning.

PREP TIME 5 MINUTES **YIELD** 4 THIGHS
SERVING 1 THIGH

INGREDIENTS

- 2 bunches rainbow chard or swiss chard
- 4 Tbsp olive oil, divided
- 6–8 rosemary sprigs
- ⅓ cup garlic cloves, frozen to prevent burning
- 4 bone-in, skin-on chicken thighs
- 1 lemon, ends trimmed, quartered, deseeded

Salt and pepper

INSTRUCTIONS

1. Separate the leaves from the stems of your rainbow chard, and slice the leaves into 1-inch strips (toss the stems). Set aside.

2. Preheat your oven to 400 degrees F and oil a flat-bottomed cast-iron pan, and drizzle 2 tablespoons olive oil on the bottom. Layer your rosemary criss-crossed, then sprinkle your garlic cloves around the rim of the pan.

3. Arrange the chicken thighs, skin-side up, on top of the rosemary and garlic, then squeeze one lemon wedge over the chicken thighs, then wedge all of them in between the four pieces of meat.

4. Drizzle again with the remaining 2 tablespoons olive oil, then sprinkle generously with salt and pepper. Move into the oven and make until chicken reaches 165 degrees F, about 30 to 40 minutes.

5. When chicken is up to temperature, set the oven to broil and bake an additional 5 to 10 minutes, or until the skin is crispy and bubbly. Remove from the oven and plate the chicken.

6. In the skillet, discard the lemon and what's left of the rosemary, then turn your burner to medium heat (add more olive oil if necessary). Add the chard a little at a time to the hot pan until it sizzles and reduces (3 to 5 minutes), then plate with the chicken.

Tip: You can buy pre-peeled garlic cloves from your local grocer and freeze them. It's so rare that you ever need fresh garlic cloves for a recipe, and this way you can have a whole bunch ready to go when you need them for a recipe like this!

Tip: You might be wondering, what's a "bunch" of chard? Basically, it's sold in "bunches" and your bunch might be larger or smaller than my bunch. I suggest defaulting to two bunches of chard and cooking as much as you'd like because one won't be enough for four people once it's reduced.

PER SERVING Net Carbs: 5g | Calories: 766 | Fat: 65g | Carbs: 6g | Protein: 40g | Fiber: 1g

STREET TACOS

Sometimes what you need while on the ketogenic diet is something you love but without all the carbs. These street tacos hit the spot with cheddar cheese shells filled with lime-infused steak and all the fixings.

PREP TIME 20 MINUTES **YIELD** 8 TACOS
SERVING 2 TACOS

INGREDIENTS

SALSA
- ½ cup diced tomato (about 1 tomato)
- ½ cup yellow onion finely diced (about ¾ onion)
- ⅛ cup fresh chopped cilantro
- ½ jalapeño, diced and deseeded
- ½ Tbsp lime juice
- ⅛ tsp sea salt

TACO
- 4 cups shredded mild cheddar cheese
- 2 lb skirt steak
- ½ cup coconut oil, melted
- 1 lime (zest plus 2 Tbsp juice)
- 1 Tbsp minced garlic
- 1 tsp grated fresh ginger
- 1 tsp red pepper flakes
- tsp sea salt

GARNISH: Shredded lettuce, cheddar cheese, avocado, red cabbage, cilantro

INSTRUCTIONS

1. About 3 hours before dinner, prepare the salsa by combining all ingredients in a glass bowl and covering with plastic wrap. Store in the refrigerator while it marinates. Note: Use less jalapeño if you'd like a milder salsa.
2. When it's dinnertime, remove your steak from the fridge. In a large bowl, combine the coconut oil, lime juice and zest, garlic, ginger, red pepper flakes and salt. Mix.
3. Add the steak and rub with the marinade (the coconut oil will harden after you're done, and that's OK).
4. Let the meat marinate for about 20 minutes at room temperature while you follow the next steps.
5. Preheat oven to 400 degrees F to start making the shells. Arrange two baking sheets with parchment paper and create eight 5-inch circles using ½ cup of mild cheddar cheese for each.
6. Add both sheets to the top rack of your oven and bake for about 15 to 20 minutes, or until edges and middle are browned.
7. Quickly use scissors to cut the parchment paper into four squares, separating each shell, then drape them over the side of a large bowl to form the shell shape. Let cool.
8. Transfer the steak to a large saute pan or skillet set over medium-high heat. You do not need to oil the pan thanks to the coconut oil in the marinade. Don't attempt to grill the steak, a flat-bottomed skillet cooking is necessary for continued cooking marination. If it doesn't fit, cut in half against the grain. If some of your marinade is still stuck to the bowl, spoon it out into the pan to cook with the steak.
9. Sear the steak on both sides until it's cooked to your desired doneness, 4 to 5 minutes per side.
10. Slice your steak against the grain into bite-size pieces, then toss for just a minute with the hot marinade one more time.
11. Fill the taco shells with the hot, saucy steak, top with the salsa you prepared earlier, then with your favorite garnishes.
Tip: If you're in a bind for time, you can make (slightly uglier) shells in the microwave, but due to size constraints, you'll probably be making them one at a time. Simply form them into circles on parchment paper (about 5 inches) and microwave on high for about 2 minutes. Make sure they're crispy around the edges and mostly cooked in the middle (may still be slightly soft). Then take them out quickly and drape them over the edge of a large bowl until they cool. Once cooled and hard, peel off the parchment paper and dab with paper towels to remove excess oil.

PER SERVING Net Carbs: 6g | Calories: 724 | Fat: 65g | Carbs: 7g | Protein: 43g | Fiber: 1g

CINNAMON BURGERS

For these burgers, the secret isn't "in the sauce," it's in the seasoning. So put together whatever hamburger ground you enjoy, then coat each side with a hearty layer of this mix. Don't worry about overdoing it; this will make the perfect amount for four hamburgers.

PREP TIME 10 MINUTES **YIELD** 4 BURGERS
SERVING 1 BURGER

INGREDIENTS

- 4 (5-oz) ground beef patties (about 1¼ lb)
- ½ Tbsp chili powder
- ½ Tbsp onion powder
- ½ Tbsp garlic salt
- ½ tsp cinnamon
- Pinch of freshly ground black pepper
- 1 romaine lettuce head, leaves separated, washed

GARNISH

Cheese, tomato, red onions, mayo, mustard, no-sugar-added ketchup.

INSTRUCTIONS

1. Preheat oven or grill to 400 degrees F.
2. In a bowl, combine the chili powder, onion powder, garlic salt, cinnamon and pepper.
3. Sprinkle the mixture over both sides of each patty.
4. Cook the patties on the grill or on a grated cast-iron pan until they reach your desired doneness. If desired, add cheese and cover until melted.
5. Serve on a bed of romaine leaves for wrapping, and add your favorite keto-friendly burger condiments.

Tip: A rare burger is 140, medium-rare is 145, medium is 160, well-done is 170. Also, watch out for high-sugar ketchup. Big-brand ketchups contain 5 grams of carbohydrates, mostly sugar, in 1 tablespoon. Most small-batch ketchups have 1 to 2 grams.

PER SERVING Net Carbs: 0g | Calories: 406 | Fat: 33g | Carbs: 1g | Protein: 24g | Fiber: 1g

WHITE GARLIC SKILLET PIZZA

Skillet pizza is super fast to make, it's filling and it curbs any white pizza cravings you might be having. If you're feeling daring, sprinkle a little grilled chicken on top too.

PREP TIME 10 MINUTES **YIELD** 1 PIZZA
SERVING 1 PIZZA

INGREDIENTS

- 1 Tbsp garlic-infused olive oil
- 1 cup shredded cheese (pizza blend)
- 1 cup shredded mozzarella cheese
- 2 Tbsp ghee or unsalted butter
- ¼ cup mascarpone cheese
- 1 Tbsp heavy cream
- 1 tsp finely minced garlic
- 2 pinches salt
- Pinch lemon pepper seasoning
- ¼ cup diced broccoli, pre-steamed, drained

GARNISH
Shaved Asiago cheese
Lemon pepper seasoning

INSTRUCTIONS

1. Over medium heat, in a medium nonstick skillet, add olive oil and shimmy the pan until it covers the bottom. Add the pizza blend cheese first and use a spatula to form into a circle with clean edges. The blended cheese is less likely to stick to the pan than the plain mozzarella. Add the mozzarella cheese on top and use the spatula again to keep it in a circle shape, about 7 to 8 inches wide.

2. Cook for 4 to 5 minutes until it gets crispy. You'll know by sliding a silicone spatula under all the edges and bottom. If it breaks apart, it's not ready. Once it's ready, you'll be able to wiggle the spatula under all the sides and the middle, and easily tip the pan to slide the crust out of the skillet and onto a plate to cool.

3. One by one while stirring, add the ghee, mascarpone cheese, heavy cream, garlic, salt, and lemon pepper seasoning to the hot pan reduced to medium-low, and cook for 5 minutes, or until it begins to bubble. Don't overcook or it may begin to separate.

4. Drizzle half the mixture over the crust. Add the chopped, steamed broccoli to the other half of the bubbling mixture in the skillet and toss, then add the broccoli to the pizza, discarding the extra sauce. Sprinkle shaved Asiago cheese and extra lemon pepper seasoning over the top, then slice into quarters with a pizza-cutter and serve.

Tip: A mozzarella crust can take practice. The biggest mistake people make is trying to make too thick of a crust, which never fully cooks, and then it takes forever to cook and ends up burning the bottom. Your crust should only be a thin, even layer of cheese that covers all the holes but doesn't pile an inch high. Also, this pizza may be small, but it's mighty. All the fats in the mozzarella cheese will keep you nice and full.

PER SERVING Net Carbs: 7g | Calories: 480 | Fat: 48g | Carbs: 8g | Protein: 29g | Fiber: 1g

Sheet Pan
GARLIC STEAK & STUFFED MUSHROOMS

A quick sear is all that's needed before you put together this simple sheet-pan meal featuring two tasty dinner staples: steak and mushrooms. The mushrooms are filled to the brim with butter and garlic, contained by a light layer of shredded Swiss cheese.

PREP TIME 15 MINUTES **YIELD** 2 PLATES **SERVING** 1 STEAK & 6 MUSHROOMS

INGREDIENTS

- 2 small ribeye steaks (about ½ lb each)
- ⅛ tsp garlic powder
- Salt & pepper
- 12 baby bella mushrooms, cleaned and destemmed
- 6 Tbsp salted butter
- ½ cup shredded Swiss cheese
- Tbsp minced garlic
- 1 Tbsp ghee

INSTRUCTIONS

1. Preheat oven to 350 degrees F.
2. Rub the skirt steaks with garlic powder and generously sprinkle with salt and pepper. Let rest for about 15 minutes at room temperature.
3. In the meantime, grease a baking sheet, then add mushrooms bottom-side up to the sheet pan. Add ½ tablespoon butter to each mushroom, then divvy up the garlic between them. Sprinkle salt and pepper over each mushroom.
4. Add the mushrooms to the oven and bake for about 10 minutes. In the meantime, begin cooking the steak.
5. Over medium heat in a large skillet, melt ghee. Sear steaks about 4 minutes on each side, covered, then remove from heat.
6. Turn the oven to a broil setting, then make room on your baking sheet to add the steak to your pan of mushrooms. Sprinkle the cheese over your mushrooms as well. Broil for about 5 minutes, then serve.

PER SERVING Net Carbs: 3g | Calories: 1,191 | Fat: 104g | Carbs: 5g | Protein: 60g | Fiber: 2g

Spicy SMOKED PAPRIKA WINGS

This recipe is a step up from your typical buffalo wing, thanks to a helping of smoked paprika that gives an extra kick.

PREP TIME 15 MINUTES **YIELD** 16 WINGS **SERVING** 4 WINGS

INGREDIENTS

- 16 fresh chicken drumsticks and flats
- 1 Tbsp extra-virgin olive oil
- 6 Tbsp salted butter
- 1 garlic clove, minced
- ⅓ cup cayenne pepper sauce (example: Frank's Hot Sauce)
- ¼ tsp smoked paprika
- ¼ tsp salt
- ⅛ tsp freshly ground black pepper

GARNISH

Blue cheese

INSTRUCTIONS

1. Preheat oven to 400 degrees F, and cover a baking sheet with an oven-safe wire rack.
2. Place the wings on the rack (this will make them extra-crispy and evenly cooked), and rub with olive oil, then sprinkle generously with salt and pepper.
3. Bake for about 45 minutes, or until crispy and at least 165 degrees F.
4. While your chicken wings are baking, add the garlic and butter to a small saucepan over medium-low heat until hot and melted. Once melted, add the rest of the ingredients and mix together.
5. When the wings are cooked, toss them in a bowl with sauce until coated. Garnish lightly with crumbled blue cheese if desired.

PER SERVING Net Carbs: 1g | Calories: 403 | Fat: 33g | Carbs: 1g | Protein: 30g | Fiber: 0g

LEMON & HERB BAKED HADDOCK

This simple and delicious haddock dish is smothered with and baked in a dish of butter and herbs.

PREP TIME 10 MINUTES **YIELD** 4 FILLETS **SERVING** 1 FILLET

INGREDIENTS

- 4 (8-oz) haddock or other white fish fillets (fresh or defrosted)
- 1 cup salted butter
- 1 Tbsp garlic, minced
- 1 tsp fresh chopped dill
- 1 tsp fresh chopped marjoram
- 1 tsp fresh chopped lemon balm
- 1 lemon, quartered
- Salt and pepper

INSTRUCTIONS

1. Preheat oven to 400 degrees F. Grease four single-serve au gratin baking dishes with butter, or use a baking dish that can fit all four haddock fillets.

2. Add the fillets to your baking dishes, then generously sprinkle with salt and pepper.

3. In the microwave or in a skillet, melt the butter together with the garlic.

4. Pour the butter mixture over the fish evenly, then sprinkle with the fresh dill, marjoram and lemon balm.

5. Bake for 10 to 12 minutes, or until flakey, then baste with the butter mixture, squeeze a fresh lemon wedge over each dish and serve on the side.

PER SERVING Net Carbs: 1g | Calories: 610 | Fat: 48g | Carbs: 1g | Protein: 43g | Fiber: 0g

CAULIFLOWER ELOTE

Mexican grilled corn (aka elote) is a delicious grilled "street food" that's covered in mayo, cotija cheese, cajun pepper and other fixings. This is a keto spin on that dish that's filling enough for a vegetarian main course.

PREP TIME 5 MINUTES **YIELD** 6 CUPS **SERVING** 1 CUP

INGREDIENTS

- 2 medium heads cauliflower
- 4 Tbsp melted ghee or butter
- ½ cup mayonnaise
- 1 cup grated cotija cheese (or fresh Parmesan), about 4 oz
- 1 tsp chili powder
- ¼ tsp cayenne pepper
- ⅛ tsp garlic powder
- 1 lime, quartered
- Salt & pepper

GARNISH

Fresh chopped cilantro

INSTRUCTIONS

1. Preheat grill to 400 degrees F.
2. Remove leaves from the cauliflower and cut the stem so it sits flat. Rub the cauliflower with melted ghee or butter, then sprinkle generously with salt and pepper.
3. Grill the cauliflower for about 30 minutes, then remove and chop finely (think: corn-sized).
4. Toss with mayonnaise, then sprinkle with cotija cheese, chili powder, cayenne pepper, garlic powder and a squeeze of lime. Garnish with fresh chopped cilantro and lime wedges if desired.

PER SERVING Net Carbs: 4g | Calories: 302 | Fat: 28g | Carbs: 6g | Protein: 7g | Fiber: 2g

Sides

YOU CAN COMPLEMENT ANY MEAL WITH THESE EASY, AND DELICIOUS, EXTRAS.

Cheesy MASHED CAULIFLOWER

What would a dinner be without a twist on the unofficial keto vegetable, cauliflower?! This cauliflower is smothered and baked in a cheesy sauce that you can cook in a few hours or set to cook while you're out for the afternoon. Serve with a juicy ribeye for a complete meal.

PREP TIME 10 MINUTES **COOK TIME** 2.5 HOURS ON HIGH **YIELD** 8 CUPS **SERVING** 1 CUP **SLOW COOKER SIZE** 6-QUART

INGREDIENTS
- 6 Tbsp butter
- 1 tsp xanthan gum
- ½ cup chicken broth
- 1 tsp poultry seasoning
- ½ tsp paprika
- 1 tsp salt
- ½ tsp freshly cracked black pepper
- ½ cup heavy whipping cream
- 1 cup whole-milk sour cream
- 1 small yellow onion, finely diced
- 2 heads cauliflower, chopped (discard stems)
- 3 cups shredded cheddar cheese

INSTRUCTIONS

1. Heat your butter and chicken stock by stove or microwave and slowly whisk in xanthan gum to create a slurry that will help thicken the sauce of this dish.

2. Pour into a bowl with the rest of the ingredients, except the cheddar cheese and cauliflower. Mix, then add in the cauliflower, then the cheddar cheese. Pour into the slow cooker.

3. Cook on high for 2½ hours, then use a large fork or potato masher to mash.

PER SERVING Net Carbs: 6g | Calories: 382 | Fat: 34g | Carbs: 8g | Protein: 12g | Fiber: 2g

WHOLE CURRY SPICED CAULIFLOWER

Bursting with flavor, the cauliflower heads can be quartered for a side or sliced tall into cauliflower "steaks" and grilled afterward if you leave them slightly undercooked. Otherwise, serve alongside poultry or seafood as a side dish.

PREP TIME 5 MINUTES **COOK TIME** 4 HOURS ON HIGH OR 6 HOURS ON LOW **YIELD** 8 QUARTERS **SERVING** 1 QUARTER **SLOW COOKER SIZE** 6-QUART

INGREDIENTS

- 2 whole small cauliflower heads, trimmed to sit flat
- 1 cup chicken broth
- ½ cup ghee or salted butter, melted
- 1 Tbsp curry powder
- 2 tsp ground cumin
- 2 tsp ground coriander
- ½ tsp sea salt

INSTRUCTIONS

1. Pour chicken broth in the bottom of the slow cooker to help cook the cauliflower.
2. Place the small cauliflowers standing up with flowers at the top and stem on the bottom so they don't tip over.
3. Rub the cauliflower with ghee, then sprinkle the spices over the cauliflower, rubbing with a gloved hand all over the cauliflower head until even.
4. Cook on high for 4 hours or on low for 6 hours. Broil for a few minutes when it's done to add crisp, or serve as-is.

PER SERVING Net Carbs: 1g | Calories: 162 | Fat: 15g | Carbs: 3g | Protein: 2g | Fiber: 2g

GARLIC & HERB RADISHES

In the words of Julia Child, "With enough butter, anything is good!" Radishes are the new potatoes—they're root vegetables, but without the starch. In fact, radishes take on a very similar flavor to potatoes when cooked right, and being slow-cooked in garlic and ghee (the oil that comes from butter) is exactly right! Serve beside a juicy steak or warm on top of a crispy salad.

PREP TIME 5 MINUTES **COOK TIME** 2–3 HOURS ON HIGH **YIELD** 3 CUPS **SERVING** ½ CUP **SLOW COOKER SIZE** 6-QUART

INGREDIENTS

- 16 oz radishes (after de-stemming, trimming and cleaning)
- 10 whole garlic cloves
- ½ cup ghee, melted
- Salt and pepper, to taste

GARNISH
- Mixed fresh herbs, chopped
- Freshly grated Parmesan cheese

INSTRUCTIONS

1. Slice the radishes into quarters and add to the slow cooker along with garlic cloves. Drizzle the melted ghee, then generously sprinkle salt and pepper over everything and toss together until coated.
2. Slow-cook on high for 2 to 3 hours, or until radishes are fork-tender and garlic cloves are soft enough to squeeze. Season with salt and pepper to your taste preference, then garnish generously with a mix of your favorite chopped herbs and Parmesan cheese, if desired.

PER SERVING Net Carbs: 3g | Calories: 200 | Fat: 20g | Carbs: 4g | Protein: 1g | Fiber: 1g

GARLIC & ONION NUT MIX

These low-carb, slow-roasted nuts will complete your keto snack cabinet. Simply slow-roast raw nuts in spices, then jar them up for later snacking. You can also use other nuts, but these were chosen based on their low carb counts.

PREP TIME 5 MINUTES **COOK TIME** 3 HOURS ON LOW, THEN 1 HOUR ON HIGH **YIELD** 4 CUPS **SERVING** ½ CUP **SLOW COOKER SIZE** 6-QUART

INGREDIENTS

- 2 cups raw almonds
- 2 cups raw pecans
- 2 cups raw walnuts
- 2 Tbsp ghee, melted
- 2 Tbsp fresh rosemary
- 2 tsp salt
- 1 tsp onion powder
- ¾ tsp garlic powder
- ¼ tsp smoked paprika

INSTRUCTIONS

1. In a slow cooker, add the nuts, then add ghee and toss. Add the rosemary, salt, onion powder, garlic powder and paprika, then toss again. Slow-cook on low for 3 hours, then 1 hour on high uncovered.

2. Remove and drain on a paper towel and let dry, or bake in the oven for 10 minutes at 350 degrees F until dry. Add salt and pepper to taste. Store in an air-tight container in a cabinet for up to two weeks.

PER SERVING Net Carbs: 3g | Calories: 537 | Fat: 52g | Carbs: 12g | Protein: 13g | Fiber: 9g

VEGGIE MEDLEY

Pop these keto-approved veggies into your slow cooker for a couple of hours to prepare a fresh veggie side to your protein main course. Add more olive oil or ghee to your liking.

PREP TIME 10 MINUTES **COOK TIME** 2 HOURS ON HIGH **YIELD** 8 CUPS **SERVING** ½ CUP **SLOW COOKER SIZE** 6-QUART

INGREDIENTS

- 2 red bell peppers, sliced into large 2" chunks
- 2 green bell peppers, sliced into large 2" chunks
- 1 small yellow onion, sliced into large 2" chunks
- 2 medium 10" yellow squash, ½" slices
- 2 medium 10" zucchini, ½" slices
- ¼ cup thinly sliced garlic cloves
- 2 Tbsp olive oil
- ¼ cup fresh chopped herbs (thyme, oregano, tarragon)
- ½ tsp salt
- ¼ tsp freshly ground black pepper
- 1 tsp lemon juice

INSTRUCTIONS

1. Add the bell peppers, onions, squash, zucchini, garlic, olive oil and fresh herbs to the slow cooker and toss. Cook on high for 2 hours.
2. Toss with salt and pepper and a light squeeze of lemon juice, then serve.

PER SERVING Net Carbs: 4g | Calories: 53 | Fat: 4g | Carbs: 5g | Protein: 1g | Fiber: 1g

Simple BROCCOLI

A simple side of broccoli is a common accoutrement to steak and chicken on a ketogenic diet. Plus, this recipe is great for meal prep.

PREP TIME 5 MINUTES **COOK TIME** 2–3 HOURS ON HIGH **YIELD** 6 CUPS **SERVING** ¾ CUP **SLOW COOKER SIZE** 6-QUART

INGREDIENTS

- 2 lb chopped broccoli (or 8–10 cups)
- ½ cup ghee (opposite page), melted (or olive oil)
- 1 tsp onion powder
- ½ tsp garlic powder
- ½ tsp salt
- ¼ tsp freshly ground black pepper
- 1 cup shredded cheddar cheese

INSTRUCTIONS

1. Add the broccoli to the slow cooker. Toss with olive oil, then add spices and toss again.
2. Cook on high for 2 to 3 hours depending on your desired doneness. Add the cheese and cook for an additional 15 minutes until melted, then serve.

PER SERVING Net Carbs: 5g | Calories: 200 | Fat: 17g | Carbs: 8g | Protein: 5g | Fiber: 3g

Spicy SAUSAGE BOLOGNESE

This spicy Bolognese sauce only gets better the longer it cooks, though be sure to stir every so often. While carrots aren't at the top of the list of keto-friendly veggies, they're a token ingredient of Bolognese and this recipe uses a minimal amount. You can omit them, though they do help tame the acidity of the tomatoes. Serve over zucchini noodles or cauliflower rice.

PREP TIME 20 MINUTES **COOK TIME** 6–8 HOURS ON LOW **YIELD** 6 CUPS **SERVING** ½ CUP **SLOW COOKER SIZE** 6-QUART

INGREDIENTS

- 2 Tbsp olive oil
- 1 small onion, chopped
- 4 cloves garlic, minced
- 1 small carrot, chopped
- 2 lb ground mild Italian sausage
- Pinch ground nutmeg
- Pinch ground cloves
- 2 Tbsp tomato paste
- ½ cup heavy cream
- 28 oz crushed tomatoes
- 1 tsp dried oregano
- 1 tsp dried thyme
- 1 tsp dried basil
- 2 bay leaves
- ½ tsp salt
- ½ tsp freshly ground black pepper

GARNISH

- Parmesan, shaved
- Fresh parsley

INSTRUCTIONS

1. In a large skillet, heat olive oil over medium-high, then add the onions, garlic and carrots and cook for 1 minute. Add ground Italian sausage and cook until browned.

2. Add the nutmeg, ground cloves, tomato paste and mix, then add the heavy cream and cook over a simmer until reduced almost completely, about 10 minutes.

3. Add to the slow cooker along with the crushed tomatoes, oregano, basil, thyme, bay leaves, salt and pepper and cook on low for 6 to 8 hours. Serve over zucchini noodles or cauliflower rice.

PER SERVING Net Carbs: 6g | Calories: 264g | Fat: 20g | Carbs: 8g | Protein: 14g | Fiber: 2g

SOUR CREAM & ONION CAULIFLOWER

Chips may be off the menu for a ketogenic diet, but you can recreate your favorite flavors in many ways, including this sour cream and onion cauliflower dish. Serve alongside your favorite protein.

PREP TIME 10 MINUTES **COOK TIME** 2.5 HOURS ON HIGH **YIELD** 4 CUPS **SERVING** ¾ CUP **SLOW COOKER SIZE** 6-QUART

INGREDIENTS

- 2 medium heads cauliflower
- 6 Tbsp ghee, melted
- 1 tsp onion powder
- 1 Tbsp dehydrated onion flakes
- ½ tsp freshly ground black pepper
- ½ tsp salt
- 1 cup sour cream
- ¼ cup chopped chives

INSTRUCTIONS

1. Chop the cauliflower into bite-size pieces, discarding the stems, then add to the slow cooker.

2. Drizzle melted ghee over cauliflower, then add the onion powder, onion flakes, black pepper and salt to the slow cooker and toss.

3. Cook on high for 2½ hours, or until fork-tender. Remove the cauliflower from the slow cooker (leave any extra liquid behind). Toss in a bowl with sour cream and fresh chives, then garnish with more freshly ground black pepper to taste. Serve warm or refrigerate and serve cold later.

PER SERVING Net Carbs: 6g | Calories: 246 | Fat: 23g | Carbs: 9g | Protein: 3g | Fiber: 3g

KETO DIPPING CHIPS

Have you really made a bowl of fresh guacamole if you have no chips to dip in it? Since tortillas are off the menu, these dipping chips made of cheese crisp up as a perfect dipping chip.

PREP TIME 5 MINUTES **COOK TIME** 20 MINUTES
YIELD ABOUT 64 CHIPS **SERVING** 8 CHIPS

INGREDIENTS

- 4 cups cheddar cheese
- ½ tsp sea salt
- ½ tsp onion powder
- ½ tsp garlic powder
- ¼ tsp cumin
- ¼ tsp paprika
- ¼ tsp chili powder

INSTRUCTIONS

1. Preheat oven to 400 degrees F and line a large baking sheet with parchment paper, leaving a little extra on the side to make it easy to pull up and out of the pan when you're done.
2. In a bowl, combine cheese and spices, then spread it out over the baking sheet and form into a rectangle, making the edges as straight as you can.
3. Bake in the oven for about 15 to 20 minutes, or until visibly crispy, then remove from the oven. Lift the cheese out of the pan with the sides of the parchment paper and place on a cool countertop. (If your cheese is soft and droopy, it needs to be cooked longer.)
4. After about 1 minute of cooling, you should be able to use a pizza cutter to cut your rectangle of cheese into triangles. The chips will harden as they cool.

PER SERVING Net Carbs: 2g | Calories: 167 | Fat: 14g | Carbs: 2g | Protein: 9g | Fiber: 0g

LOADED FAUX-TATO

Potatoes are off-limits on the keto diet, but you won't miss them with this creamy cauliflower and avocado whip, topped with the works!

PREP TIME 20 MINUTES **COOK TIME** 15 MINUTES
YIELD 4 FAUX-TATO HALVES **SERVING** 1 FAUX-TATO HALF

INGREDIENTS

- 3 cups chopped cauliflower, steamed
- 8 oz bacon, cooked and crumbled
- 2 large, ripe avocados
- 1½ tsp sea salt
- ¼ tsp freshly cracked pepper
- 2 Tbsp heavy cream
- ½ tsp onion powder
- ½ cup butter, melted

GARNISH (OPTIONAL)
- Shredded cheddar
- Green onions
- Chives
- Sour cream

INSTRUCTIONS

1. Preheat oven to 375 degrees F.
2. Slice an avocado in half the long way, twist and split apart. Remove and discard the pit, then carefully remove the avocado meat, keeping the shell intact, and set the meat and shell aside.
3. In a blender or with an immersion blender, blend the steamed cauliflower (drained if wet), avocado, salt, pepper, cream, onion powder, butter and half of the crumbled bacon. Use a spoon to taste and see if it fits your salt preferences. Depending on your avocados, you may need more.
4. Spoon the mix into the avocado shells, then bake in the oven for about 15 minutes, or until hot all the way through.
5. Remove from the oven and top with the remaining crumbled bacon and all of your favorite fixings. Enjoy—but don't eat the avocado shell!

PER SERVING Net Carbs: 3g | Calories: 618 | Fat: 56g | Carbs: 10g | Protein: 22g | Fiber: 7g

GARLIC CHEESE STICKS

Next time you're chowing down on some sauce-drenched veggie noodles, pair them with these protein-rich garlic cheese sticks to curb your breadstick cravings.

PREP TIME 5 MINUTES **COOK TIME** 20 MINUTES **YIELD** 16 STICKS **SERVING** 4 STICKS

INGREDIENTS

- 2 cups whole-milk shredded mozzarella cheese
- 1 Tbsp minced garlic
- 1 tsp Italian seasoning
- 1 tsp salt
- 1 Tbsp salted butter
- 1 Tbsp, plus ¼ cup grated Parmesan cheese

INSTRUCTIONS

1. Preheat oven to 400 degrees F and line a small baking sheet (9-by-13-inch) with parchment paper, leaving a little outside so you can easily lift out when done.
2. Spread out the mozzarella cheese evenly. Add garlic, Italian seasoning, salt and 1 tablespoon Parmesan cheese and shuffle until mixed.
3. Bake in the oven for about 20 minutes, or until the moisture has baked out and the cheese looks crispy throughout.
4. Remove from the oven and lift the cheese from the pan using the parchment and place on a cool surface.
5. Brush with butter and sprinkle with remaining Parmesan cheese. Use a pizza cutter to slice into eight cheesesticks, then slice down the middle the opposite way to make 16 dippable sticks. Serve with marinara as a side or alongside veggie noodles.

PER SERVING Net Carbs: 3g | Calories: 232 | Fat: 19g | Carbs: 3g | Protein: 14g | Fiber: 0g

CILANTRO LIME CAULIFLOWER RICE

This "rice" cooks quickly in a skillet with fresh lime juice, garlic and butter, tossed with freshly chopped cilantro. Use a food processor or grater to quickly make cauliflower rice, or use a knife to chop pieces as small as you can. Since this side dish is low in protein, it's great paired with a taco bowl or a seared, garlicky steak.

PREP TIME 5 MINUTES **COOK TIME** 5 MINUTES
YIELD 4 CUPS **SERVING** 1 CUP

INGREDIENTS

- 3 Tbsp ghee or butter
- 2 tsp minced garlic
- 3 cups cauliflower, riced
- 1 tsp salt
- 2 Tbsp lime juice, plus zest of 1 lime
- ½ cup sliced scallions
- 1 tsp fresh cracked pepper
- ½ cup chopped cilantro

INSTRUCTIONS

1. In a large skillet, melt the ghee or butter. Add the minced garlic for about 15 seconds until fragrant (careful not to burn), then add the cauliflower rice and salt. Mix and cover for about 5 minutes, or until the cauliflower is tender.
2. Toss with the lime juice, scallions, pepper and cilantro. Serve.

PER SERVING Net Carbs: 3g | Calories: 126 | Fat: 14g |Carbs: 4g | Protein: 1g | Fiber: 1g

CAULI MAC AND CHEESE WITH BACON

This "mac" and cheese recipe is stick-to-the-roof-of-your-mouth good and made with roasted cauliflower. Roasting the fresh (not frozen!) cauliflower ahead of time removes excess moisture, which creates the perfect consistency when tossed with the cheese sauce.

PREP TIME 15 MINUTES **COOK TIME** 1 HOUR
YIELD 4 CUPS **SERVING** 1 CUP

INGREDIENTS

- 3–4 cups fresh cauliflower chopped into bite-size pieces (about 1 large head)
- 1 Tbsp olive oil
- 1 tsp mustard powder
- ½ tsp onion powder
- ½ tsp salt
- Freshly ground pepper to taste
- 6 slices thick-cut bacon

CHEESE SAUCE

- 4 Tbsp salted butter
- ½ cup chicken broth
- ½ cup heavy cream
- ½ tsp xanthan gum
- 1 cup cheddar cheese

INSTRUCTIONS

1. Preheat oven to 400 degrees F and prepare a large baking sheet.
2. Spread the cauliflower across the baking sheet, drizzle with olive oil and toss to coat.
3. Sprinkle the mustard powder, onion powder and salt over the cauliflower and toss again. Crack a little pepper over the top for good measure.
4. Chop your bacon into 1-inch squares, then lay them around and on top of the cauliflower evenly.
5. Bake for about 30 minutes, then use a spatula to toss and mix. Bake for another 15 minutes, then use a spatula to toss and mix again. At this point, there should be little to no moisture left in the bottom of the dish.
6. Meanwhile get your ingredients for the sauce ready while it bakes.
7. Flip and toss again, and bake for the final 15 minutes. During the last 15 minutes, you'll make your sauce.
8. In a sauté pan, melt the butter over medium heat. Add the broth and heavy cream until warm, then add the xanthan gum. Stir until it begins to bubble.
9. Remove from heat and add the cheddar cheese slowly. Stir continuously until the cheese melts completely. If you haven't already, remove the cauliflower from the oven.
10. Pour the cheese over your cauliflower mix and toss. Enjoy while it's hot.

PER SERVING Net Carbs: 4g | Calories: 439 | Fat: 41g | Carbs: 6g | Protein: 14g | Fiber: 2g

SQUASH RIBBON PASTA
in Lemon Cream Sauce

This recipe uses shaved zucchini and summer squash "ribbons" as the main course—much tastier than their finicky zoodle counterparts.

PREP TIME 15 MINUTES **COOK TIME** 10 MINUTES
YIELD 2 SERVINGS **SERVING** 2

INGREDIENTS

- 2 zucchini (medium, 8")
- 2 yellow summer squash (medium, 8")
- 1 Tbsp olive oil
- 1 tsp garlic powder
- ⅛ tsp freshly cracked pepper
- ⅛ tsp lemon juice
- 1 Tbsp parsley (divided)
- ½ cup chicken broth
- 1½ cups heavy cream
- 2 tsp garlic, minced
- 1 lemon (quartered)
- 1 Tbsp ghee
- Salt and pepper to taste

INSTRUCTIONS

1. Wash your yellow squash and zucchini, then use a vegetable peeler over a bowl to create a mix of short and long, thin ribbons. Do this until you hit the seeds, then stop peeling and discard the veggie bellies or save for a different recipe. This should make about 4 heaping cups of "ribbons." Toss the ribbons with the olive oil, garlic powder, pepper, lemon juice and 1 tablespoon of freshly chopped parsley. Set aside.

2. In a medium sauté pan over medium heat, add the chicken broth and bring to a boil. Add the heavy cream, minced garlic and lemon (quartered), then let simmer for 5 to 10 minutes on low until reduced in half. Stir frequently. When done, set aside.

3. While the sauce is reducing, heat the ghee in a skillet. Cook the ribbons for about 5 minutes, or until soft but still crisp.

4. Once the sauce has reduced in half, discard the lemons and any seeds (or squeeze if you want more lemon flavor), season with salt and pepper to taste, then add the ribbons, toss and garnish with the remaining freshly chopped parsley. Serve alongside grilled chicken, fish or shrimp.

PER SERVING Net Carbs: 4g | Calories: 375 | Fat: 37g | Carbs: 4g | Protein: 7g | Fiber: 0g

CAJUN SPAGHETTI SQUASH PASTA

The natural sweetness of spaghetti squash complements this Southern-style cream sauce so well it feels like a cheat. Spaghetti squash does have a modest amount of carbs (7 total and 5.5 net per cup), which is why this dish works well in moderation as a side to your favorite carbless proteins like chicken, halibut or shrimp.

PREP TIME 5 MINUTES **COOK TIME** 45 MINUTES
YIELD 3 CUPS **SERVING** ¾ CUP

INGREDIENTS

- 1 large spaghetti squash
- 2 cups heavy cream
- 3 Tbsp butter
- 1 tsp garlic salt
- 1 Tbsp Cajun seasoning
- ½ tsp cayenne pepper

INSTRUCTIONS

1. Cut the spaghetti squash in half. Remove the seeds and discard, then place the squash cut-side down in a glass baking dish with a little bit of water. Bake for 35 to 45 minutes, or until cooked. Use a fork to loosen the "noodles" and put aside. (Alternatively, you can microwave the dish for 10 to 15 minutes, although this method is more likely to overcook the squash than the oven.)

2. Over medium heat in a medium skillet, heat up the cream, butter, garlic salt, Cajun seasoning and cayenne pepper. When it begins to simmer, add the spaghetti squash and reduce to a simmer over medium-low. The sauce should reduce in half over the course of 20 minutes.

3. When the sauce is ready it should stick to the squash, and it will thicken more as it cools. Serve with your favorite protein for a full meal, and crack fresh pepper over the top as a garnish.

PER SERVING Net Carbs: 8g | Calories: 501 | Fat: 57g | Carbs: 9g | Protein: 1g | Fiber: 1g

BACON BROCCOLI CHEDDAR SALAD

This simple side salad is perfect for a summer day next to a bunless burger. Simply make your eggs ahead of time or buy them pre-boiled for a super-fast dish. Also great for meal prep.

PREP TIME 15 MINUTES **COOK TIME** 20 MINUTES
YIELD 6 CUPS **SERVING** 1 CUP

INGREDIENTS

- 8 oz bacon
- 1 head broccoli
- 6 eggs, boiled, peeled
- ½ cup mayonnaise
- ½ tsp salt
- ¼ tsp black pepper
- ⅛ tsp paprika
- ⅛ tsp garlic powder
- ¼ cup finely shredded cheddar

INSTRUCTIONS

1. Preheat oven to 400 degrees F and arrange the bacon on a large baking sheet. Bake for 20 minutes until crispy, then remove and drain on paper towels. Once it's cooled, crumble the bacon and set aside.

2. Cut your head of broccoli into fourths, then roughly chop into bite-size pieces and add to a medium mixing bowl.

3. Chop your eggs into bite-size pieces, then add them to the same bowl as the broccoli, followed by the mayo, salt, pepper, paprika and garlic powder. Mix vigorously until all the yolks have softened and blended into the salad. Adjust to taste, depending on the size of the broccoli head.

4. Next, add the crumbled bacon and shredded cheddar and mix again. Serve chilled.

PER SERVING Net Carbs: 3g | Calories: 398 | Fat: 32g | Carbs: 5g | Protein: 22g | Fiber: 2g

90-SECOND KETO BREAD

This keto-friendly bread only uses five ingredients and bakes in 90 seconds! Use this as a tasty base for your next keto sandwich or toast to curb your carb cravings.

PREP TIME 5 MINUTES **COOK TIME** 2 MINUTES
YIELD 1 CUP **SERVING** 1 CUP

INGREDIENTS

- 1 Tbsp butter or oil
- 1 medium/large egg
- ½ tsp baking powder
- ⅓ cup blanched almond flour
- 1 pinch salt

INSTRUCTIONS

1. Microwave the butter in a microwave-safe mug until melted, about 15 seconds. Swirl the mug to make sure it is fully coated with melted butter.

2. In the mug, combine the egg, baking powder, almond flour and salt and whisk until smooth.

3. Microwave the mug until set, about 90 seconds. Let cool for 2 minutes before slicing. Serve.

PER SERVING Net Carbs: 6g | Calories: 408 | Fat: 36g | Carbs: 10g | Protein: 15g | Fiber: 4g

NOTES

Dessert

GET YOUR SWEET FIX AND KEEP YOURSELF IN KETOSIS WITH THESE MOUTH-WATERING DELIGHTS!

MEYER LEMON CUSTARD

Using the slow cooker as a water bath, these custard snacks are practically impossible to curdle or otherwise mess with. Finally, an easy way to make custard!

PREP TIME 5 MINUTES **COOK TIME** 2.5 HOURS ON LOW **YIELD** 4 JARS **SERVING** 1 JAR **SLOW COOKER SIZE** 6-QUART

INGREDIENTS

- 8 large egg yolks
- 3 Meyer lemons (zest and 4 Tbsp juice)
- 1 cup unsalted butter, melted
- ¼ cup powdered erythritol
- 10 drops stevia glycerite
- 1 Tbsp vanilla extract

REQUIRED: 4 small Mason jars

INSTRUCTIONS

1. Place the lids of your Mason jars on the bottom of the slow cooker, top-side up. You'll use these to keep the Mason jars raised off the bottom.
2. Blend all ingredients together, then pour into the jars. Place the jars on top of the lids so they're lifted about ½ inch from the bottom. Fill the slow cooker with water until it reaches the middle of the jars (any higher and they will tip).
3. Cook on low for 2½ hours with a paper towel or tea towel under the lid to prevent condensation. Remove the jars and eat right away, or dry off the lids, cover the jars and cool in the refrigerator for later.

PER SERVING Net Carbs: 2g | Calories: 528 | Fat: 55g | Carbs: 2g | Protein: 6g | Fiber: 0g

COCONUT BLONDIES TWO WAYS

Serving these hot out of the crock with some fresh whipped cream makes this delectable dish similar to bread-pudding. If you refrigerate it, though, you can slice it into small fudgy bites that store well and make controlling portion sizes easier.

PREP TIME 5 MINUTES **COOK TIME** 2 HOURS ON HIGH
YIELD 15 SQUARE-ISH SLICES **SERVING** 1 SLICE
SLOW COOKER SIZE 6-QUART

INGREDIENTS

- 2 cups finely ground almond flour
- 1 cup coconut flour
- 2 (14-oz) cans coconut milk, cream only (refrigerate first to separate), 1 cup total cream
- 1 cup shredded coconut, unsweetened
- 1 cup powdered erythritol
- 1 tsp baking powder
- 10 drops stevia glycerite
- 1 egg
- 1 cup butter, room-temperature

INSTRUCTIONS

1. Mash and mix all ingredients with a wooden spatula until smooth. Small lumps of butter or coconut cream are fine.

2. Grease the slow cooker, then add the mixture and cook on high for 2 hours, rotating halfway through. Eat hot like a bread pudding, or cool it in the refrigerator for a more dense, chewy bite.

PER SERVING Net Carbs: 5g | Calories: 335 | Fat: 32g | Carbs: 9g | Protein: 5g | Fiber: 4g

Giant CHOCOLATE CHIP COOKIE

For the keto chocolate chip cookie lover in your life, this dessert tastes so very close to the real thing! Hot, it resembles a more cake-like texture, and after it cools, it's closer to a brownie!

PREP TIME 10 MINUTES **COOK TIME** 2 HOURS ON HIGH
YIELD 20 SQUARE-ISH SLICES **SERVING** 1 SLICE
SLOW COOKER SIZE 6-QUART

INGREDIENTS

- 1 cup butter, softened
- 1 cup "brown sugar" erythritol (e.g. Swerve®, Lakanto®)
- 1 tsp baking soda
- ¼ tsp salt
- 2 large eggs
- 2 Tbsp heavy cream
- 2 tsp vanilla extract
- 1 tsp almond extract
- 15 drops stevia glycerite
- 3 cups finely ground almond flour
- 1 cup keto-friendly dark chocolate chips (e.g. Lily's™, Guittard®)

INSTRUCTIONS

1. In a bowl with a hand mixer, cream together the softened butter, erythritol, baking soda and salt. Add the eggs, heavy cream, vanilla extract, almond extract and stevia glycerite and blend again, then use a spatula to mix in the almond flour then the chocolate chips.

2. Line the slow cooker with aluminum foil or parchment paper and spray or grease with butter. Pour in the batter, then slow-cook for 2 hours on high, rotating the insert halfway through to prevent burning on one side. Turn off heat when edges are browned and a knife comes out clean. Lift out of the insert using the edges of your liner and cool on a counter for 30 minutes. Once cooled, slice and serve.

PER SERVING Net Carbs: 3g | Calories: 219 | Fat: 21g | Carbs: 4g | Protein: 5g | Fiber: 1g

PUMPKIN PIE PUDDING

To save carbs on the crust, this pumpkin pie is served like pudding in a bowl and can be topped with fresh whipped cream and nutmeg for added fat.

PREP TIME 5 MINUTES **COOK TIME** 3 HOURS ON LOW **YIELD** 6 CUPS **SERVING** ½ CUP **SLOW COOKER SIZE** 6-QUART

INGREDIENTS

- 8 large eggs
- 32 oz 100% pumpkin purée
- 1 cup powdered erythritol
- 15 drops stevia glycerite
- 1 Tbsp maple or vanilla extract
- 2 tsp pumpkin pie spice
- Pinch salt
- ½ cup melted butter or ghee, plus 2 Tbsp for greasing

INSTRUCTIONS

Grease the sides of the slow cooker with 2 tablespoons butter or ghee. Add all ingredients and mix. Cook on low for 3 hours, then scoop and serve.

Per Serving Net Carbs: 5g | Calories: 147 | Fat: 11g | Carbs: 7g | Protein: 5g | Fiber: 2g

CHOCOLATE AVOCADO BROWNIES

These chewy, fudgy brownies are the perfect morsels for a chocolate craving, with some added healthy fats from the ghee and avocado.

PREP TIME 10 MINUTES **COOK TIME** 1.5–2 HOURS ON HIGH **YIELD** 20 SQUARE-ISH SLICES **SERVING** 1 SLICE **SLOW COOKER SIZE** 6-QUART

INGREDIENTS

- 1 cup ripe avocado, cubed (about 1 avocado)
- 4 Tbsp ghee or butter, melted
- 1 cup powdered erythritol
- 15 drops stevia glycerite
- 4 Tbsp cacao or cocoa powder
- ½ tsp baking soda
- ⅛ tsp salt
- 2 cups finely ground almond flour
- 1 cup keto-friendly chocolate chips (e.g. Lily's™, Guittard®)

INSTRUCTIONS

1. In a mixing bowl, add the ripe avocado (must be soft and ripe), butter, erythritol, glycerite, cacao or cocoa powder, baking soda and salt. Use a hand mixer to cream together.

2. Use a spatula to mix in the almond flour then chocolate chips.

3. Line the slow cooker with aluminum foil or parchment so you can easily remove the brownies when they're done. Spray or grease with butter, then pour in batter.

4. Cook on high for 1½ to 2 hours, rotating the crock halfway through to prevent uneven cooking. Remove from the crock using your liner, and place on a cool countertop for 3 minutes to cool.

PER SERVING Net Carbs: 2g | Calories: 119 | Fat: 11g | Carbs: 4g | Protein: 3g | Fiber: 2g

RASPBERRY CHEESECAKE

This easy cheesecake only takes a few ingredients and a few minutes, and it's addictively delicious!

PREP TIME 10 MINUTES **COOK TIME** 2 HOURS ON HIGH **YIELD** 12 SLICES **SERVING** 1 SLICE **SLOW COOKER SIZE** 6-QUART

INGREDIENTS

- 24 oz cream cheese, softened
- 4 large eggs
- 1 cup powdered erythritol
- 1 tsp vanilla extract
- 5 drops stevia glycerite
- 20 raspberries (plus more for garnish)

INSTRUCTIONS

1. Line the slow cooker with aluminum foil or parchment paper and grease. Add the cream cheese to a mixing bowl, then use a hand mixer to mix, adding each ingredient slowly, starting with the eggs, then the erythritol, vanilla and stevia glycerite. Add five roughly chopped raspberries and mix.

2. Pour into the slow cooker and cook on high for 2 hours, using a paper towel under the cover to catch any condensation. Remove the crock and refrigerate for at least 2 hours. Use the liner to lift the cheesecake out, remove the liner, top with remaining raspberries, then slice and serve.

PER SERVING Net Carbs: 2g | Calories: 226 | Fat: 22g | Carbs: 2g | Protein: 6g | Fiber: 0g

BERRY COBBLER

This berry cobbler can be prepared in less than five minutes and creates a bursting, juicy dessert everyone will enjoy.

PREP TIME 5 MINUTES **COOK TIME** 2 HOURS ON HIGH **YIELD** 8 CUPS **SERVING** ½ CUP **SLOW COOKER SIZE** 6-QUART

INGREDIENTS

- 16 oz strawberries, halved
- 12 oz raspberries
- 12 oz blackberries
- 6 oz blueberries
- 2 tsp xanthan gum
- 15 drops stevia glycerite
- Pinch ground cinnamon
- 2 cups finely ground almond flour
- 1 Tbsp granulated erythritol (optional)
- Pinch salt
- 8 Tbsp unsalted butter, sliced into pats

GARNISH

Fresh whipped cream for added fats, optional

INSTRUCTIONS

1. In a slow cooker, add berries and toss with xanthan gum, stevia glycerite and ground cinnamon. Mix the almond flour, erythritol and salt together, then sprinkle over the berry mixture and place pats of butter all over.
2. Cook on high for 2 hours with a paper towel under the lid to prevent condensation from dripping, then scoop and serve.

PER SERVING Net Carbs: 5g | Calories: 188 | Fat: 17g | Carbs: 7g | Protein: 3g | Fiber: 2g

LEMON BUTTERCREAM COOKIE SANDWICHES

Buttercream frosting is as natural to a ketogenic dessert as butter itself. This scrumptious sweet lemon dessert uses erythritol as a sweetener, which, despite its clinical sounding name, is a natural sugar alcohol.

PREP TIME 30 MINUTES **COOK TIME** 15 MINUTES
YIELD 12 COOKIE SANDWICHES
SERVING 1 COOKIE SANDWICH

INGREDIENTS

COOKIES
- 1/3 cup unsalted butter, room temperature
- ½ cup granulated erythritol sweetener
- 1 tsp vanilla extract
- 1 cup fine almond flour
- 1 lemon (zest only)
- Pinch of salt

BUTTERCREAM FROSTING
- ½ cup butter, room temperature
- 1 cup powdered erythritol
- 1 Tbsp lemon juice
- 2 Tbsp heavy whipping cream
- 1 tsp lemon zest

INSTRUCTIONS

1. Preheat oven to 300 degrees F.
2. To create the cookie dough, combine the butter, granulated erythritol and vanilla extract with a hand mixer. Next, add the almond flour, lemon zest and salt and mix thoroughly with your hands to form a ball of dough.
3. Line a large baking sheet with parchment paper, then roll your dough down on the right-hand side of the sheet using a rolling pin, creating a flat circle about ¼ inch thick.
4. Use a 2-inch round cookie-cutter to create circles, then leave the circles and clean up the scraps. Do this again on the left-hand side until you've used up the batter. It should make 12 cookies. You can use a silicone candy or cookie mold to make 12 cookies; this will help the cookies retain their round shape when they cook in the oven. They will flatten into larger cookies without the mold.
5. Bake in the oven for 15 minutes (20 if you are using the silicone mold), then remove and let the cookies cool completely. They may be very soft when they come out and will harden once they cool. Refrigerate to quicken the process.
6. While the cookies are baking, make your buttercream frosting. Mix the room temperature butter and confectioners erythritol sweetener together with a hand mixer, then add the lemon juice, heavy whipping cream and lemon zest. Refrigerate to thicken.
7. When your cookies are cooled, use a frosting sleeve or zipper storage bag with the corner cut off to pipe the buttercream onto the middle of half of the cookies, then top each with another cookie and smoosh together. Serve.

PER SERVING Net Carbs: 1g | Calories: 176 | Fat: 18g | Carbs: 2g | Protein: 2g | Fiber: 1g

Ooey Gooey BUTTER PIE

Traditional butter cake and chess pie are off-limits on the ketogenic diet due to their high sugar content, but this hybrid dessert hits every buttery, vanilla note you're craving.

PREP TIME 40 MINUTES **COOK TIME** 30 MINUTES
YIELD 8 SLICES **SERVING** 1 SLICE

INGREDIENTS

CRUST
- 1 cup finely ground almond flour
- 1 Tbsp powdered erythritol
- 1 large egg
- 4 Tbsp melted unsalted butter
- Pinch of salt

PIE FILLING
- 8 oz softened cream cheese
- ½ cup melted unsalted butter
- ¾ cup powdered erythritol
- 6 drops stevia glycerite
- Pinch of salt
- 2 large eggs
- Heavy whipping cream, whipped and piped on top of pie (optional)

INSTRUCTIONS

1. Preheat oven to 350 degrees F and grease a 9-inch pie plate.
2. In a bowl, combine the crust ingredients, then press into the bottom of the pie plate.
3. In a separate bowl, use a hand mixer and cream together the pie filling, starting with the cream cheese and butter, then erythritol, stevia glycerite, salt and eggs at the end.
4. Pour the pie filling over the crust in the pie plate, then bake for approximately 30 minutes, or until the top is brown. (It's OK if it's slightly jiggly, but a fork should come out clean when you poke it.)
5. Once your butter pie is removed from the oven, refrigerate for at least 2 hours to set (really—it's worth the wait), then serve.

PER SERVING Net Carbs: 2g | Calories: 217 | Fat: 21g | Carbs: 3g | Protein: 5g | Fiber: 1g

MASCARPONE BERRY FRUIT SALAD

Fruit salad wouldn't be keto without added fats, and nobody will complain when you toss it in a sweet, rich mascarpone cream. Perfect for a single serving dessert or multiply it to bring as your contribution to the neighborhood block party.

PREP TIME 5 MINUTES **YIELD** 4 SERVINGS
SERVING ½ CUP

INGREDIENTS

- 2 cups mixed berries (strawberries, raspberries, blackberries, blueberries)
- ½ cup mascarpone, softened
- ½ tsp vanilla extract
- 2 drops stevia glycerite
- 1 Tbsp heavy cream
- Pulp of 1 vanilla bean (optional)

INSTRUCTIONS

1. In a bowl, use a hand blender to mix the softened or warmed mascarpone, vanilla extract, stevia glycerite, heavy cream and vanilla bean pulp. The mix should be light like a dressing; if not, microwave for 15 seconds.
2. Toss the berries into a bowl and lightly toss. Refrigerate for 30 minutes and enjoy.

PER SERVING Net Carbs: 4g | Calories: 162 | Fat: 16g | Carbs: 7g | Protein: 3g | Fiber: 3g

STRAWBERRY SHORTCAKE

The secret to this fresh and tasty low-carb strawberry shortcake is in the almond flour crust, which tastes like shortbread when paired with fresh strawberries.

PREP TIME 10 MINUTES **YIELD** 4 SHORTCAKE BOWLS
SERVING 1 SHORTCAKE BOWL

INGREDIENTS

- 2 cups heavy whipping cream
- ½ cup almond meal
- 2 Tbsp unsalted butter, melted
- 4 drops stevia glycerite
- ½ tsp vanilla extract
- 16 medium strawberries, chopped

INSTRUCTIONS

1. In advance, prepare your whipped cream by using a hand mixer and a frozen bowl to whip heavy whipping cream into a thick whipped cream.
2. In a bowl, combine the melted butter, almond meal, stevia glycerite and vanilla extract. Mix into a dough, then press into the bottom of four small dessert glasses.
3. Top each with chopped strawberries, then with whipped cream.
4. Refrigerate for at least 30 minutes to set the crust, then serve.

PER SERVING Net Carbs: 8g | Calories: 572 | Fat: 58g | Carbs: 10g | Protein: 6g | Fiber: 2g

Vanilla Bean COCONUT ICE CREAM

No ice-cream maker is required for this dessert—in fact, you can eat it right away if you so desire! Coconut cream, which is rich in fats, takes center stage in this healthy, ketogenic treat. Stevia glycerite is non-bitter and adds the perfect touch of sweetness.

PREP TIME 10 MINUTES **YIELD** 3 CUPS **SERVING** ¾ CUP

INGREDIENTS

- 3 (14-oz) cans unsweetened coconut milk
- 1 fresh vanilla bean
- 1 tsp vanilla extract
- 6 drops stevia glycerite
- 3 Tbsp heavy cream

INSTRUCTIONS

1. Note: The day before you plan to make this recipe, put your cans of coconut milk in the refrigerator and freeze a large mixing bowl.
2. Slice your vanilla bean pod down the middle to open, then use the flat edge of your knife to scrape out and save the inside pulp. Discard your vanilla bean or save for another recipe.
3. Open three cans of refrigerated coconut milk and use a spoon to remove the cream from the top—which should be solid from refrigeration—and add to your frozen mixing bowl.
4. Use a hand blender to mix the cream until fluffy and smooth, then add vanilla bean pulp, vanilla extract, stevia glycerite and heavy cream, then blend again.
5. Spoon into a small bread pan or baking dish. Lining the dish first will help if you decide to reblend the ice cream later for an even creamier texture.
6. Eat right away, or freeze overnight and allow at least 1 hour to thaw before eating.

PER SERVING Net Carbs: 3g | Calories: 315 | Fat: 31g | Carbs: 3g | Protein: 0g | Fiber: 0g

Raspberry Lemon BUTTER CAKE

Imagine if raspberry lemonade and an ooey gooey Southern butter cake made a baby: that's what you can eat for dessert (and breakfast!) all week when you make this cake.

PREP TIME 10 MINUTES **COOK TIME** 40 MINUTES
YIELD 10 SLICES **SERVING** 1 SLICE

INGREDIENTS

- 3 cups finely ground almond flour
- ¾ cup granulated erythritol sweetener
- 1 lemon, zest and 2 Tbsp juice
- ½ tsp xanthan gum
- ½ tsp baking powder
- ½ tsp baking soda
- Pinch of salt
- 1 Tbsp flaxseed flour (alternate: coconut flour)
- ¾ cup butter, softened
- 1 tsp vanilla extract
- 2 eggs
- 1 cup fresh raspberries

INSTRUCTIONS

1. Preheat oven to 350 degrees F and grease a 9-inch pie plate.
2. In a large bowl, mix the almond flour, sweetener, lemon zest, xanthan gum, baking powder, baking soda, salt and flaxseed flour until thoroughly combined.
3. Add the butter, vanilla extract and eggs to the dry ingredients and mix thoroughly into a batter. Add the raspberries last and gently fold into the batter.
4. Spoon the batter into your greased pie plate, then bake for 30 to 40 minutes.
5. Allow to cool, then slice and serve. Refrigerate to store, and heat up as a snack all week!

PER SERVING Net Carbs: 4g | Calories: 341 | Fat: 32g | Carbs: 9g | Protein: 9g | Fiber: 5g

SALTED LIME CUPCAKES

For the flavor of a lime margarita in your mouth, try these cupcakes with a cream cheese icing. For a dairy-free and more tropical flavor, substitute cream cheese for unsweetened and chilled cream of coconut.

PREP TIME 20 MINUTES **YIELD** 12 CUPCAKES
SERVING 1 CUPCAKE

INGREDIENTS
CUPCAKES
- 4 Tbsp salted butter, softened
- ¼ tsp vanilla extract
- 1 large egg
- 5 drops stevia glycerite
- 1 lime, zest plus ½ tsp juice
- ½ tsp baking powder
- 2 tsp granulated erythritol
- ½ cup fine almond flour

FROSTING
- 8 oz cream cheese, room temperature
- 4 Tbsp unsalted butter, room temperature
- 1 tsp vanilla extract
- 1 lime, zest plus 1 Tbsp juice
- 2 Tbsp powdered erythritol
- 5 drops stevia glycerite
- Optional: Flaked sea salt (like Malden's)

INSTRUCTIONS
1. Preheat oven to 375 degrees F and line a mini muffin tin with 12 mini muffin/cupcake liners.
2. In a bowl, use a hand mixer to blend the softened butter, vanilla extract, egg, stevia glycerite, lime juice and zest. Use a spatula to mix in the baking powder, erythritol and almond flour until smooth.
3. Spoon the batter (will be somewhat thick) into each of the cupcake liners. They should fill about ¾ of the way.
4. Pop in the oven for about 10 minutes, or until browned on top, then remove from the oven and cool for at least 1 hour.
5. In a bowl, use a hand mixer to blend all of the frosting ingredients—except for the salt— starting with the cream cheese, then butter, then adding the rest.
6. Finally, spoon or pipe the frosting onto each of the cupcakes and chill for at least 1 hour in the fridge (they're best served cold).
7. Garnish with flaked sea salt, any remaining lime zest and lime wedges.

PER SERVING Net Carbs: 1g | Calories: 168 | Fat: 17g | Carbs: 2g | Protein: 3g | Fiber: 1g

FRUIT SALAD

Berries are the fruits lowest in sugars and carbs, but they're also low in fats. To make a keto fruit salad, this recipe uses creme fraiche to add a little fat. Enjoy ½ cup for dessert or even breakfast.

PREP TIME 5 MINUTES **YIELD** 7 CUPS **SERVING** ½ CUP

INGREDIENTS

- 2 cups fresh sliced strawberries
- 2 cups fresh raspberries
- 2 cups fresh blackberries
- 1 cup fresh blueberries
- 1 cup creme fraiche
- 10 drops stevia glycerite
- 1 tsp vanilla extract

GARNISH

Mint or Strawberry Mint

INSTRUCTIONS

Wash and dry the berries. Then mix together the creme fraiche, stevia and vanilla extract. Add the berries and toss gently, then serve.

PER SERVING Net Carbs: 5g | Calories: 82 | Fat: 6g | Carbs: 8g | Protein: 1g | Fiber: 3g

NOTES

NOTES

NOTES

NOTES

NOTES

NOTES

NOTES

NOTES

INDEX

A

Aioli, garlic, 13
Almond
    butter, 36
    extract, 100
    flour, 16, 20, 24, 94, 99, 100, 102, 104, 105, 106, 110, 111
    meal, 108
Amino, liquid, 46
Arrowroot powder, 52
Artichoke hearts, 50
Avocado, 13, 39, 45, 61, 69, 87, 102
    oil, 52

B

Bacon, 13, 15, 19, 22, 23, 29, 30, 39, 49, 87, 90, 93, 94
Baking powder, 16, 20, 24, 94, 99, 110, 111
Baking soda, 20, 100, 102
Beef
    chuck roast, 45, 57
    flank steak, 43
    ground, 29, 52, 61, 66, 70
    ribeye steak, 72
    skirt steak, 69
    steak, 59
Berries, 35
    blackberries, 107, 112
    blueberries, 104, 107, 112
    raspberries, 36, 37, 103, 104, 107, 112
    strawberries, 37, 104, 107, 108, 112
Broccoli, 19, 43, 46, 65, 71, 83, 93, 94
Broth
    beef, 43, 45, 57
    chicken, 12, 19, 33, 45, 48, 54, 57, 78, 79, 90, 91
Brown sugar, keto-friendly, 58
Brussels sprouts, 48

C

Cabbage, 46
    red, 69
Cacao powder, 102
Carrots, 84
Chard
    rainbow, 68
    swiss, 68
Cauliflower, 12, 22, 46, 47, 51, 61, 67, 75, 78, 79, 85, 87, 89, 90
Celery, 28
Cheese, 70
    Asiago, 60, 71
    blue, 28, 65, 73
    cheddar, 12, 13, 14, 19, 23, 29, 30, 49, 52, 61, 65, 66, 69, 71, 78, 83, 86, 87, 90, 93, 94
    cotija, 75
    cream, 15, 16, 20, 24, 29, 30, 35, 50, 65, 103, 106, 111
    four-cheese Mexican blend, 66
    goat, 45
    Gouda, 13
    Gruyere, 33
    mascarpone, 71, 107
    mozzarella, 24, 28, 31, 47, 50, 55, 60, 62, 71, 88
    Parmesan, 12, 32, 53, 55, 60, 62, 75, 80, 84, 88
    pepper jack, 59
    ricotta, 55
    Swiss, 33, 72
Chia seeds, 37
Chicken, 56
    breasts
        boneless, 44, 62
        deli slices, 55
    drum sticks, 73
    ground, 28, 67
    rotisserie, 30, 65
    tenderloins, 48
    thighs, 49, 50, 51, 53, 54, 68
    wings, 32
Chocolate
    baker's, 34
    chips, keto-friendly, 100, 102
Cocoa powder, 102

Coconut
   aminos, liquid, 43
   flakes, unsweetened, 17
   flour, 15, 20, 67, 99
   milk, 44, 99, 109
   oil, 17, 34, 69
   shredded, uunsweetened, 98
Crème fraiche, 112
Cucumbers, pickling, 38

E

Egg(s), 12, 13, 14, 15, 16, 19, 20, 21, 23, 24, 28, 39, 47, 54, 55, 67, 93, 94, 98, 99, 100, 101, 103, 106, 111
Erythritol
   "brown sugar", 100
   granulated, 20, 35, 37, 104, 105, 110, 111
   powdered, 16, 20, 34, 98, 99, 101, 102, 103, 105, 106, 111

F

Flaxseed flour, 20

G

Ghee, 12, 13, 14, 15, 19, 21, 32, 44, 51, 57, 67, 72, 75, 79, 80, 81, 83, 85, 89, 91, 101, 102
Ginger, 43, 67, 69

H

Haddock filets, 42, 74
Ham
   cubed, 12, 14
Heavy (whipping) cream, 12, 14, 15, 16, 19, 23, 24, 34, 36, 48, 51, 67, 71, 78, 84, 87, 90, 91, 92, 100, 104, 105, 106, 107, 108, 109
Herbs, 80
   arugula, 13
   basil, 31, 37, 44, 55
   chives, 22, 85, 87
   cilantro, 45, 51, 67, 69, 69, 75, 89
   dill, 38, 42, 74
   lemon balm, 74
   marjoram, 74
   mint, 36, 112
      strawberry, 112
   oregano, 54, 57, 82
   parsley, 32, 53, 57, 84, 91
   rosemary, 68, 81
   sage, 18
   tarragon, 82
   thyme, 18, 57, 82

J

Juice
   lemon, 16, 37, 42, 67, 74, 82, 91, 105, 110
   lime, 44, 45, 69, 89

K

Ketchup, low, no-sugar, 29, 70

L

Lakanto, 58, 100
Lemon, 16, 42, 48, 54, 56, 68, 74, 91, 98, 105, 110
   juice, see Juice
Lettuce, 69, 70
Lime, 69, 75, 111
   juice, see Juice
Liquid smoke, 18, 58

M

Maple extract, 18, 101
Mayonnaise, 30, 50, 59, 70, 75, 93, 94
Mushrooms
   baby bella, 72
   white, 53
Mustard, 29, 70
   Dijon, 19, 59
   yellow, 63

N

Nuts
   almonds, 17, 81
   pecans, 81
   walnuts, 15, 17, 81

O

Olives, black, 31
Onion, 23, 31, 59, 84
  green onions, 30, 49, 61, 87, 89
  red, 29, 45, 55, 70
  white, 44, 67
  yellow, 12, 14, 22, 29, 51, 53, 63, 69, 78, 82
Orange
  extract, 24
  zest, 24, 52

P

Pancetta, 48
Pepper
  chilies, green, 22, 45, 52
  green, 12, 14, 31, 47, 53, 55, 59, 63, 82
  jalapeño, 14, 30, 61, 69
  red, 12, 23, 43, 46, 47, 50, 53, 55, 63, 82
  yellow, 47, 63
Peppermint extract, 34
Pickling salt, 38
Poppy seeds, 16
Pork
  butt, 58
  ground, 18, 46
  rinds, 62
  shoulder, 58
Pumpkin, 44, 101

R

Radishes, 80

S

Sauce
  barbecue, sugar-free, keto-friendly, 49
  cayenne pepper, 73
  hot, 28, 45, 65
  marinara, no-sugar, 31, 60
  Sriracha, 46
  tomato, 58, 70
    low-carb, 62
    sugar-free, 53
    keto-friendly, 47, 55
  Worcestershire, 57, 58
Sausage
  ground, 23
  Italian, 31, 47, 55, 63, 84
  kielbasa, 12
  Polish, 12
Sea salt, 61, 69, 79, 86, 87
  flaked, 111
Sesame
  oil, 46
  seeds, 29, 46
Shallots, 19
Sour cream, 20, 61, 78, 85, 87
Spices
  allspice, 18
  basil, 53, 84
  bay leaves, 84
  Cajun seasoning, 22, 92
  cayenne pepper, 28, 33, 52, 58, 61, 75, 92
  celery salt, 57
  chili powder, 45, 52, 61, 66, 70, 75, 86
  cinnamon, 15, 17, 19, 20, 24, 37, 44, 61, 67, 70, 104
  cloves, 84
  coriander, 44, 79
  cumin, 45, 52, 61, 66, 67, 79, 86
  curry powder, 44, 51, 67, 79
  dill weed, 57
  fennel seeds, 18
  Garam Masala, 67
  garlic
    powder, 30, 50, 52, 56, 57, 58, 60, 65, 72, 75, 81, 83, 86, 91, 93, 94
    salt, 57, 62, 70, 92
  ginger, 44
  Herbes de Provence, 56
  Italian seasoning, 47, 60, 62, 88
  lemon pepper seasoning, 71
  mustard powder, 90
  mustard seeds, 38
  nutmeg, 15, 20, 33, 84
  onion flakes, dried, 85

onion powder, 28, 32, 52, 57, 58, 61, 66, 70, 81, 83, 85, 86, 87, 90
oregano, 52, 53, 54, 57, 61, 84
paprika, 22, 65, 78, 86, 93, 94
    smoked, 28, 45, 52, 58, 61, 66, 73, 81
parsley, 57
peppercorns, 38
poultry seasoning, 78
pumpkin pie spice, 101
red pepper flakes, 18, 32, 43, 44, 52, 53, 69
thyme, 57, 84
turmeric, 67
Spinach, 50
Squash
    spaghetti, 92
    yellow, 82, 91
Stevia glycerite, 15, 16, 17, 18, 20, 36, 37, 43, 52, 98, 99, 100, 101, 102, 103, 104, 106, 107, 108, 109, 111, 112
Sweetener
    brown sugar, sugar-free, 24
    vanilla, sugar-free, 24
Swerve, 24, 58, 100

T

Tamari, 43, 46
Tomato(es), 31, 49, 69
    crushed, 51, 67, 84
    diced, 53
        chili-ready, 29
        with chilies, 61
    paste, 52, 84

V

Vanilla
    bean, 107, 109
    extract, 15, 16, 20, 24, 34, 35, 36, 98, 100, 101, 103, 105, 107, 108, 109, 111, 112
Vinegar
    apple cider, 38, 58, 63
    rice wine, 46

W

Wine, red, 53

X

Xanthan gum, 33, 52, 78, 90, 104, 110

Z

Zucchini, 62, 82, 91

CONVERSION CHART

AN EASY-TO-REFERENCE GUIDE FOR WHEN YOU TAKE YOUR DIET ABROAD.

VOLUME

¼ teaspoon	1.25 mL
½ teaspoon	2.75 mL
1 teaspoon	5 mL
1 tablespoon	15 mL
¼ cup	60 mL
⅓ cup	80 mL
½ cup	120 mL
⅔ cup	160 mL
¾ cup	180 mL
1 cup	240 mL
1 quart	1 liter
1½ quarts	1.5 liters
2 quarts	2 liters
2½ quarts	2.5 liters
3 quarts	3 liters
4 quarts	4 liters

WEIGHT

1 ounce	30 grams
2 ounces	55 grams
3 ounces	85 grams
4 ounces (¼ pound)	115 grams
8 ounces (½ pound)	225 grams
16 ounces (1 pound)	455 grams
2 pounds	910 grams

LENGTH

⅛ inch	3 mm
¼ inch	6 mm
½ inch	13 mm
¾ inch	19 mm
1 inch	2.5 cm
2 inches	5 cm

TEMPERATURES

Fahrenheit	Celsius
32°	0°
212°	100°
250°	120°
275°	140°
300°	150°
325°	160°
350°	180°
375°	190°
400°	200°
425°	220°
450°	230°
475°	250°
500°	260°

Topix Media Lab
For inquiries, call 646-838-6637

Copyright 2019 Topix Media Lab

Published by Topix Media Lab
14 Wall Street, Suite 4B
New York, NY 10005

Printed in the U.S.

All rights reserved. No part of this publication may be reproduced in any form or by any electronic or mechanical means, including information storage and retrieval systems, without permission in writing from the publisher, except by a reviewer, who may quote brief passages in a review.

Certain photographs used in this publication are used by license or permission from the owner thereof, or are otherwise publicly available. This publication is not endorsed by any person or entity appearing herein. Any product names, logos, brands or trademarks featured or referred to in the publication are the property of their respective trademark owners. Topix Media Lab is not affiliated with, nor sponsored or endorsed by, any of the persons, entities, product names, logos, brands or other trademarks featured or referred to in any of its publications.

Note to our readers
The information in this publication should not be substituted for, or used to alter, medical therapy without your doctor's advice. For a specific health problem, consult your physician for guidance.

The information in this publication has been carefully researched, and every reasonable effort has been made to ensure its accuracy. Neither the publication's publisher nor its creators assume any responsibility for any accidents, injuries, losses or other damages that might come from its use. You are solely responsible for taking any and all reasonable and necessary precautions when performing the activities detailed in its pages.

ISBN: 978-1-948174-51-0

CEO Tony Romando

Vice President & Publisher Phil Sexton
Senior Vice President of Sales & New Markets Tom Mifsud
Vice President of Retail Sales & Logistics Linda Greenblatt
Director of Finance Vandana Patel
Manufacturing Director Nancy Puskuldjian
Financial Analyst Matthew Quinn
Brand Marketing & Promotions Assistant Emily McBride

Editor-in-Chief Jeff Ashworth
Creative Director Steven Charny
Photo Director Dave Weiss
Managing Editor Courtney Kerrigan
Senior Editor Tim Baker

Content Editor Juliana Sharaf
Art Director Susan Dazzo
Associate Photo Editor Catherine Armanasco
Associate Editor Trevor Courneen
Copy Editor & Fact Checker Benjamin VanHoose
Designer Kelsey Payne

Co-Founders Bob Lee, Tony Romando

Recipe Development Amanda C. Hughes

Indexing by R studio T, NYC

www.ingramcontent.com/pod-product-compliance
Lightning Source LLC
Chambersburg PA
CBHW081724100526
44591CB00016B/2489